RATTAN

[signature]

RATTAN

A WORLD OF ELEGANCE AND CHARM

LULU LYTLE

with ELIZABETH WILHIDE

Foreword by MITCHELL OWENS

RIZZOLI NEW YORK

New York · Paris · London · Milan

CONTENTS

FOREWORD by Mitchell Owens

PAGE 2: *The Honeymoon*, 1921 (oil on canvas) by Irish painter Sir John Lavery (1856–1941). Lavery was associated with The Glasgow Boys, a group of Scottish and Irish artists. His formative years saw him painting *en plein air*, during which time he developed a particular skill for capturing—in a post-Impressionist style—the atmosphere of people at leisure.

PAGES 4–5: The Danish actress Annette Strøyberg, relaxing on a terrace in Italy, July 1970. She was best known as the second wife of French film director Roger Vadim. His first was Brigitte Bardot.

OPPOSITE: The loggia of an Andalusian villa, designed by Laura Sartori Rimini and Roberto Peregalli of Studio Peregalli, is lined with rattan armchairs and benches. Vegetation climbs the architecture, which is painted in Pompeiian red.

Craftsmanship—in this fast-forward, surface-skimming, technology-leaping day and age—may seem quaint, but Lulu Lytle knows better. For more than two decades, this lively, wide-smiling, endlessly curious Englishwoman and enterprising cofounder of the award-winning home-furnishings firm known as Soane Britain has been a standard-bearer for the artisanal. More than many of the creative forces that I know, it is she who understands the importance of the art that is contained within that word. Skills that require the dexterity of the hand, the judgment of the eye, and the devotion to methods that have been elements of world culture for time immemorial are indeed arts. Craftsmanship has its own Michelangelos, its own Gentileschis, and its own Rembrandts—men and women who have elevated the simple to the sublime, advancing noble crafts into the future without losing any of their inherent authenticity. Nor, in fact, the possibilities.

A Southeast Asian climbing palm, rattan is a vinous plant that aspires to be a tree and, in many cases, offers many of the same creative opportunities. Masters of the craft, though, are few and far between today, but like so many of the British artisans with whom Lulu works, from blacksmiths who forge iron and steel to saddlers who sew leather upholstery, the future has become brighter. It was she who stepped in at a perilous moment in 2010 when England's very last rattan-weaving workshop was on the verge of closing its doors forever, ensuring its survival and bringing its expertise to a new audience.

In experienced hands of those artisans, the natural, sustainable fiber undergoes an almost alchemical transformation. Subjected to techniques that seem every bit as complicated (and inscrutable) as those used in lacemaking, the rattan is thoroughly moistened so that it can be manipulated—straightened and curled, crisscrossed and woven, braided and interlocked—and ultimately sculpted into objects of wonder.

Legs in emulation of fern fronds hold aloft the surface of a console table. The shade of a pendant light is coaxed into the shape of a birdcage. Row upon row of rattan is formed into a spherical table lamp that stands on a flirty base resembling a peplum. Add to this Soane's range of mirror frames, chairs, breakfast trays, barstools, drum tables, vases, and more—many of them new in spirit but an equal number anchored in or inspired by the rich past of an endlessly pliable medium, as well as custom-made originals—and it becomes clear: Lulu Lytle not only knows rattan, she is putting it on a pedestal for the world to admire anew.

INTRODUCTION: The Allure of Rattan

As a child, I was captivated by a painting that hung in my aunt's house in Oxfordshire. I had never met my grandfather and was therefore particularly fascinated by this portrait of him as a young man in Cape Town, painted by his brother. It is extraordinarily atmospheric. Of course, I didn't appreciate then that the chair he sat in was rattan, but now I wonder if those hours spent gazing at Grandpa might have subliminally instilled in me a love of wicker furniture. A little far-fetched maybe, but I am not sure how else I can explain why, in my late teens, I developed such a devotion to rattan.

I first became aware of furniture made of plant fiber while in Egypt, and saw not only the extraordinary pieces with which Tutankhamen was buried but also the ubiquitous café chairs and tables made from the date palm. Around the same time, I started buying old pieces of rattan furniture, cluttering up my long-suffering parents' house and stables with old daybeds, chairs, tables, and baskets. The crowning moment was when I arrived home triumphantly bearing an Edwardian rattan cart with a fabric canopy, designed to carry a child pulled by a large dog or small pony. It was stamped "Dryad," which I was later to discover was the most important English rattan workshop, founded in 1907 by the Arts and Crafts patron and social reformer Harry Hardy Peach.

ABOVE: Botanical illustration of the calamus rotang plant from *The Natural History of Plants: Their Forms, Growth, Reproduction, and Distribution* by Austrian botanist and author Anton Kerner von Marilaun (1831–98).

OPPOSITE: The Heywood-Wakefield Company was one of the leading American manufacturers of wicker furniture. At its peak, the company's production facilities occupied eleven acres of land in Wakefield, Massachusetts. Here, one of their delivery trucks is piled high with chairs.

PAGE 12: Weaver Phil Ayres and frame-maker Mick Gregory at the Soane Britain rattan workshop in Thurmaston, in the English county of Leicestershire.

PAGE 13: Part of Soane's Lily collection, designed in collaboration with Los Angeles–based decorator Mark D. Sikes, the Lily sofa sits in the Great House at Cobblers Cove, a charming family-owned hotel in Barbados.

My introduction to rattan manufacturing came about because of an Edwardian rattan sofa that I bought from an Irish house sale. The sofa was really gutsy in scale and of an age and condition that gave it a particular beauty. I was keen to produce a modern version of the design for Soane, and equally determined that it should be made in Britain. This proved harder than I had thought, with the British rattan companies simply importing Asian-made rattan, having given up manufacturing decades earlier. After an extensive search, a friend finally located the last British rattan workshop, Angraves, in Leicestershire.

Fortuitously, Angraves had not only been making its own large archive of designs but had also taken on some of the original Dryad designs when they ceased making rattan furniture in 1956. Angraves employed around thirty-five people, but at this point only two of them were still making furniture in the traditional way. In 2010, after we had been commissioning Angraves to make Soane

rattan designs for eight years, we received the sad news that it was going into liquidation, on the eve of its centenary. Imports from the Far East and the vagaries of furniture fashion had proved too challenging for the company. Galvanized by the need to continue to make rattan furnishings for our clients, combined with the fear that these specialized skills would soon be lost to Britain forever, I bought the raw materials and machinery from the liquidators and reemployed the two craftsmen who had been making Soane's designs. With more than ninety years combined rattan-weaving experience between them, Mick Gregory and Phil Ayres guided me in the setting up of a new workshop in Thurmaston in Leicestershire, minutes from the original locations of both Dryad and Angraves. We continued to produce the same pieces we had been making before, which would not have been possible without Mick's and Phil's extraordinary knowledge, commitment to British rattan weaving, and desire to educate the next

ABOVE: Two children in a wicker stroller on the boardwalk in Atlantic City, New Jersey, 1924. Rattan was commonly used to make baby carriages, along with other wheeled conveyances.

OPPOSITE: Palm Beach, Florida, was first developed as a glamorous holiday destination by the rail tycoon Henry Flagler. In the late 1890s, Flagler built two luxurious hotels on what was, at that time, a desolate barrier island on Florida's Atlantic coast. A moneyed elite soon began flocking to the fledgling resort during the winter months. Flagler banned motor vehicles on the island, and guests were conveyed along a pine trail between the two hotels in "Palm Beach Coaches," essentially rattan chairs attached to the front of bicycles. Here, Evalyn Walsh McLean (1886–1967) is photographed with her son, Vinson, and poodle. A mining heiress and socialite, Mrs. McLean was the last private owner of the forty-five-carat Hope Diamond.

generation of weavers. After coaxing weavers out of retirement and apprenticing a new generation, we now have fifteen frame makers, weavers, and finishers, including three generations of the same family, in our workshop.

Although rattan's popularity has ebbed and flowed over the years, it retains a certain allure that few other materials possess. Immediately evocative of warmth, relaxation, and laid-back elegance, rattan is associated with exotic travel and the glamorous lifestyles of Diana Vreeland's "beautiful people," imbuing it with great romance. There is hardly a movie star or luminary who hasn't at some point posed in a Peacock chair, while rattan recliners, lounge chairs, and sofas appear in innumerable photographs of European royalty in their orangeries and gardens or on their yachts. While rattan is synonymous with languid summer days, it has many personas: from the innocent simplicity of a child's cradle and the rose-filled rattan trug in an English glasshouse to the clean rigor of a Bauhaus interior and the more hedonistic atmosphere of Jay Gatsby's West Egg.

In more recent decades, notable rattan enthusiasts have employed the material's potential, incorporating it into their interiors and reveling in its ability to lighten the atmosphere of even the grandest architectural settings. Tastemakers such as Marella Agnelli and Bunny Mellon, both of whom were devoted to wicker, understood its value as a counterbalance to fine art and antiques and, in the

This informal portrait of the British Royal Family (left to right: King George VI, Princess Elizabeth, Princess Margaret, and Queen Elizabeth) was taken in the grounds of Windsor Castle in 1946, a year after the end of the Second World War. The rattan furniture was designed by Dryad and made in Leicester.

Bunny Mellon (1910–2014), revered for her aesthetic sensibility, was a horticulturalist, gardener, and art collector. She was a close friend of President and Mrs. Kennedy and designed the White House Rose Garden. Her credo that "nothing should be noticed" might explain her fondness for the visually understated and humble nature of wicker. Her home in Antigua was furnished with abundant fresh flowers, piles of books, and willow and rattan furniture, which contributed to the atmosphere described by her husband, the banking heir Paul Mellon, as "lived in, loved, and cheerful."

ABOVE: Taboo nightclub on Worth Avenue in Palm Beach, Florida, 1942. The stick wicker chairs, made from unprocessed rattan poles, strike a note of informality and ease. Taboo, or Ta-boo, welcomed many noteworthy guests, from John F. Kennedy and Frank Sinatra to the Duke and Duchess of Windsor. It is one of the many bars claiming to have invented the Bloody Mary, concocted by a bartender at the request of Barbara Hutton for a soothing drink after a night of carousing. It was said that "if you were not seen at Ta-boo, you were not seen in town."

OPPOSITE: A green-painted woven rattan dining table, designed by Soane, is glimpsed through curtains made from their Tendril Vine printed-linen sheer. It is less usual to find rattan tables on central column bases, the majority being designed with three or more legs.

process, turned this humble material into a signifier of high style from palazzo to poolside.

Rattan is an extraordinary plant. Like bamboo, which boasts around a thousand species and ranges from the miniature to the giant, there are some six hundred species of this Old World palm, the greater proportion of which is native to the tropical rainforests of Indonesia, Malaysia, and the Philippines, among others. Unlike bamboo, however, rattan is a vine. Its flexible spine hooks over and scrambles up through other vegetation to allow its leaves to reach the light. Admirably sustainable because it is so fast-growing (up to twenty feet per year, growing in extreme cases to almost six hundred feet in a lifetime), rattan is strong, durable, and exceptionally versatile. While bamboo canes are rigid and hollow, the tough inner core of dense rattan canes is easy to manipulate once steamed or soaked, allowing for the weaving

fluid three-dimensional forms limited only by the designer's or craftsperson's imagination.

Rattan's inherent malleability lends itself to almost any stylistic interpretation. Early modernists valued rattan because it provided a clean-lined, lightweight alternative to upholstery. Designers in the art deco style delighted in creating bold geometric shapes, while mid-century designers used this unpretentious material to produce sculptural organic forms. And that is to say nothing of the highly ornate flights of fancy, abounding in curlicues and decorative flourishes, which came out of the Victorian and Edwardian eras—everything from intricate baby carriages to wickerwork "bicycle chairs." Decades before synthetic materials became prevalent in ordinary household items, rattan was employed almost as the plastic of its day, highly rated for its flexibility yet, of course, entirely natural in origin.

OPPOSITE: This light-drenched sun porch is filled with a charming mixture of painted and natural rattan, willow, and bamboo collected over many years. An old sea captain's cottage, perched on a cliff sixty feet above Puget Sound, Washington, the house is now a summer retreat of James Sansum and Manhattan-based designer Markham Roberts, a devotee of wicker, who enthuses, "Rattan and wicker, whether vintage or new, are like instant old friends: comfortable and easy, which grow better with time."

RIGHT: This house in Capri was completely rebuilt by Studio Peregalli in the spirit of the Caprese architecture of the eighteenth and nineteenth centuries. On the main terrace, paved with salvaged slabs of volcanic stone, rattan armchairs sit under an ancient olive tree. Laura Sartori Rimini and Roberto Peregalli believe that "rattan is an interesting material, because it is sophisticated with high craftsmanship, and, at the same time, preserves its rustic, natural character. It can be used not only for the exterior but also for the interior. Another fundamental quality is that even when it is new, rattan seems immediately old and connected to the past."

Rattan—the name derives from the Malay *rotan*—is often used interchangeably with wicker. Here, an important distinction must be made. While rattan is a natural fiber, wicker is the product of the craft of weaving, not only with rattan but also with willow, reed, rush, raffia, and a host of other fibrous materials. Wicker is known to date back thousands of years. Rattan itself only came to the attention of furniture-makers in the West once trading routes to the Far East became established in the seventeenth and eighteenth centuries. At that time, it was so plentiful it was primarily used as loose packing material in ships' holds and jettisoned once the cargo was safely in harbor. It was European colonists who appreciated firsthand the advantages of rattan in hot climates: its resistance to pests, the fact that it does not warp or crack in conditions of extreme heat and humidity, its open weave that allows cooling air to circulate, and its lightness and portability.

Rattan's most recent revival has largely been design-driven. While vintage rattan pieces, particularly by named designers, continue to hold their value in auction houses, new designs are increasingly popular in contemporary interiors—from hotels and restaurants to beach houses, chalets, and city apartments. Personally, I have relished watching Soane's craftspeople experiment in the workshop, seeing the miracles they can coax out of this infinitely obliging plant. The possibilities are endless. I have particularly loved exploring rattan's potential for lighting, where

ABOVE: Woven rattan furniture by the first British rattan producer W. T. Ellmore in the great gallery of the Royal Automobile Club, on London's Pall Mall. It was most probably installed when the clubhouse first opened in 1911. The company, later known as W. T. Ellmore & Son, was first established in Leicester in 1886. This is the earliest image that I have found of a public interior in England decorated entirely with rattan.

OPPOSITE: Antique rattan chairs on a palm-filled balcony overlooking an internal courtyard with a glazed skylight designed by Gustave Eiffel. This nineteenth-century French town house in Perpignan near the Spanish border is the home of Françoise and Henri Quinta, founders of Les Toiles du Soleil, and saviors of the only surviving Catalan mill, weaving traditional striped canvas.

its mellow diffusion of light creates evocative patterns and pools of shade.

Rattan also has an importance beyond the aesthetic. A few years ago, I was astonished to discover from journalist Jonathan Foyle that scientists at the Institute for Science and Technology for Ceramics of the Italian National Research Council (ISTEC-CNR) have found that rattan makes a better substitute for human bone than other materials commonly used in bone-replacement surgery do. When heated with calcium, rattan acquires a porous texture so similar to bone structure that nerves and blood vessels will grow through it. Its flexibility allows it to move with the body, unlike metal or ceramic alloys, which are rigid. The ergonomic potential of this extraordinary plant is constantly evolving.

With every discovery I make about rattan, I am more beguiled by this material's chameleon-like qualities and the possibilities it offers designers. Unlike the soulless uniformity of more mass-produced pieces, properly made rattan furniture and lighting has an intangible atmosphere, elegance, and charm that I find endlessly irresistible.

ABOVE: *Little Girls in the Garden* or
The Basket Chair, 1885 (oil on canvas)
by French Impressionist Berthe Morisot
(1841-95). Known for her intimate
domestic scenes and her superb use of
color, Morisot often painted *en plein air*.

ABOVE: The legendary Elsie de Wolfe, dressed in gym clothes, relaxes on a rattan lounger at her home in Paris, 1935, after a workout. She followed a strict physical regime and first learned to swim at the age of sixty. At the outbreak of the Second World War, she and her husband, Sir Charles Mendl, formerly an attaché at the British Embassy in Paris, fled Paris. Subsequently, de Wolfe became known as a leading Hollywood hostess. She is still revered as "America's first decorator."

No. 254   £4.10.0
Robin Hood Settee

LEFT: Three girls pose in a Robin Hood chair made by Dryad. This Leicester-based rattan workshop, established by Harry Hardy Peach in 1907, was a major British producer of rattan furniture, exporting its goods around the world in the early decades of the twentieth century. Rattan was used for both the steam-bent frame and the woven mesh of this model.

BELOW LEFT: Dryad's extensive catalog advertised every conceivable household requirement—from armchairs to dining tables, cake stands to tea trolleys, log baskets to planters.

OPPOSITE: Soane's Pavilion chairs take inspiration from the faux-bamboo chairs commissioned, among other Chinese-inspired exotica, by the Prince of Wales (who became King George IV in 1820), to furnish The Long Gallery at the Royal Pavilion at Brighton in the late eighteenth century. This dining room has curtains made from Koro weave fabric designed by Duro Olowu for Soane Britain.

The History of Rattan

THE HISTORY OF RATTAN

Although rattan was a relative latecomer to the West, the craft of wicker dates back thousands of years. Made of woven strands of various types of plant fiber, including willow, reed, and straw, as well as rattan itself, its precise origins are necessarily a matter of conjecture, but it is thought that the technique may well have emerged at the time of the earliest agricultural settlements, when it was most likely employed to produce basic shelters, along with a variety of simple containers, such as baskets.

When it comes to the ancient civilizations of Egypt and Rome, historians are on surer ground. By around 2600 B.C., the Egyptians had discovered how easy it was to work wet reeds into various shapes and how durable the result was when it dried in the sun. Given that early cultures generally made use of what was easiest to source locally, Egyptian craftspeople probably used the swamp grasses that grew in the fertile Nile delta as their principal raw material. Elaborate wicker chairs, tables, baskets, boxes, and chests were discovered in the tombs of the pharaohs, indicating that such items had high status. Many of these were brightly colored. Tutankhamen (circa 1341–1323 B.C.) was buried with a number of wicker items, including a chair seat, a stool, and a headboard.

A rapid expansion of the wicker technique came with the Roman Empire. Plainer, paler, and more rectilinear than the Egyptian variety, Roman wicker was used to make screens, swings, and furniture, along with more everyday items. In 2000, archaeologists at Pompeii unearthed a wicker basket under a stairwell in the public baths. It contained a twenty-piece silver dinner service hastily bundled by some desperate inhabitant fleeing the eruption of Mount Vesuvius in 79 A.D.

There is also archaeological evidence of wickerwork in widespread usage in northern Europe during the Iron and Bronze Ages, which

suggests the craft developed independently there—or that prehistoric settlements were less isolated than is generally supposed. Small boats such as the coracle, or currach, were often made of wicker, waterproofed with a hide covering, as were creels, baskets, and panniers for carting heavy loads. Wicker floor mats and wattlework outer walls were typical features of Iron Age roundhouses, while a recent discovery at a farm in Cambridgeshire comprised twelve Bronze Age eel traps, almost identical in design to those still used in the marshy fenlands today. Some theorists have suggested that the woven patterns of Celtic art had their origins in wicker. Alder, ash, hazel, and birch twigs were common materials, along with willow, straw, and rush.

Although wickerwork was a common technique in northern Europe by the Middle Ages, rattan itself did not reach the West until the Age of Exploration dawned during the fifteenth century. Neither did it penetrate many Eastern territories outside those where the species was prevalent. The principal areas where rattan was grown, and still

ABOVE: Gathering rattan on Bukit Timah Road, Singapore, 1895. Due to its proximity to Indonesia, where rattan grows in abundance, and to China, where generations of craftspeople had practiced the skills of rattan weaving, Singapore became a major processor of rattan and an exporter of rattan furniture during the nineteenth century.

LEFT: This 1797 lithograph of a "Tiger of War" Chinese soldier is based on a watercolor by William Alexander (1767–1816). The soldier is bearing the traditional rattan shield, called a *téngpái*.

光緒甲午秋九月吉旦

京口駐防八旗官兵泰立

仁恩周鐵甕膏澤下施三軍糈幸沐鴻

恭頌

和甫觀察大人

德政

惠溥兵民

恭頌

和甫觀察大人

德政

懋績樹金陵器重上游半載辛勤膚受

京口駐防八旗官兵泰立

和甫觀察大人

德政

grows today, are in Australasia, notably Malaysia, Indonesia, and the Philippines, and in India and southeast Asia. Although it may be reasonable to assume that rattan, along with the craft of wicker, could well have reached mainland China before that period, given its geographical proximity, there is no firm evidence to support this. Once it did, however, sometime in the fifteenth century, rattan weaving was taken to new heights of sophistication. A defining feature of Chinese rattan, evident in a variety of highly refined artifacts from serving bowls to storage boxes, was the lightness of the woven mesh. From China, rattan weaving soon spread to Japan and Korea. The versatility of the material can be seen in the wide range of goods that was produced, from the Korean *deungpae*, a rattan shield used in martial arts, to ornamental Japanese *inrō* basketry.

Rattan truly began to come into its own with burgeoning global trade. The Dutch East India Company, founded in the early seventeenth century, established colonies and supply outposts across southeast Asia—from the Indian subcontinent to Ceylon (Sri Lanka), Indonesia, and Taiwan. The British East India Company, founded in 1657 and modeled on its Dutch counterpart, plied similar

Designed by leading architect Howard Greenley (1874–1963) in the Beaux-Arts manner, the Prince George Hotel in New York first opened in 1904 and soon became a popular gathering place in the Madison Square vicinity. The Ladies' Tearoom, pictured here in 1907, with its trellised columns and arches, and faience fountain, was filled with an impressive array of rattan and willow furniture. Following a period of closure from the late 1980s onward, the hotel reopened in 1999, offering permanent supportive housing. The restored public spaces, such as the ballroom and tearoom, are now event spaces. Greenley was also the architect of a number of grand summer houses on Long Island and in Newport.

trade routes, laying the foundations of what would later become the far-flung colonies of a vast empire. Catering to a growing European market for spices, silk, cotton, porcelain, and printed textiles, these companies, and others like them, fostered a creative cross-fertilization that was to mark East-West relations for many centuries to come.

Both the Dutch and the British were early importers of rattan from Malaysia and Indonesia. While rattan was often used as disposable packing material, jettisoned once a ship reached harbor, during the seventeenth century, its practical advantages in furniture became more apparent. Unlike upholstered seats, where bugs could linger, chair seats made of split and woven rattan were cheaper, lighter, and more hygienic. Rattan also proved to be stronger than European wicker materials. From the 1660s onward, London became an important center of caned furniture, particularly chairs; by the 1680s, tens of thousands were made every year, many of which were exported. In France, such chairs were known as *chaises anglaises* and in Germany as *englische Stühle*. At this time, there was little understanding of rattan's design potential. It was simply incorporated as a detail within furniture of post-Renaissance and baroque styles.

All this began to change around the late eighteenth century and the beginning of the nineteenth, when a taste for the exotic swept the decorative arts. In Britain, the exemplar was the Royal Pavilion at Brighton—that confection of Oriental influences built as a seaside pleasure palace for the Prince Regent, later George IV (1762–1830). During the Regency period, faux-bamboo furniture was the rage, and rattan became even more prevalent, not only in the form of

Tearoom Hotel Prince George

cane seats but also as side panels in bergères, giving furniture a lighter and airier appearance. Other cane items were also produced, including cradles and headboards. The notable English cabinetmaker Thomas Sheraton (1751–1806) recommended canework for "anything where lightness, cleanness, and durability ought to be combined."

The long reign of Queen Victoria (1819–1901), which coincided with the growth of industrialization and the global dominance of the British Empire, saw rattan furniture produced in the Far East specifically for the British and European markets. No longer incidental detailing, rattan became a familiar sight on Victorian lawns and terraces, in conservatories, and in other less formal areas of the home. At a time when prolonged stints overseas in the military or in colonial administration were commonplace, many of rattan's Victorian consumers would have experienced its practicalities firsthand. Lightweight, inexpensive, and delightfully exotic in a domesticated way, rattan furniture—from chairs and tables to planters and storage pieces—grew in popularity as the century progressed. Both the Aesthetic movement, which drew heavily on Japanese influences, and the Arts and Crafts movement, with its emphasis on simplicity of design and honest use of materials, helped to keep rattan in vogue, its malleability lending itself to the expression of very different decorative styles.

The first Western factory to employ rattan in mechanized wicker production was established by a grocer named Cyrus Wakefield

ABOVE: A sensation in its day, the interior of the Trellis Room at the Colony Club (its first location on Madison Avenue) in New York City was designed by Elsie de Wolfe in 1907. At a time when public spaces tended to be elaborately furnished and decorated, de Wolfe's use of light, pale colors (white and green were her favorites) and airy rattan and willow furniture was truly groundbreaking.

(1811–73). Married to the daughter of a shipping magnate, he came across a large bundle of rattan abandoned on a dock in Boston after its use as packing material on a ship in the 1840s. Intrigued, he took some of the rattan home and experimented with it, weaving it around the framework of a chair. His ingenious idea—to marry this otherwise disposable waste with the wicker process—was put into practice in 1851, when he sold his grocery business and founded the Wakefield Rattan Company in South Reading, Massachusetts. The furniture, baskets, and baby carriages produced by Wakefield were soon in high demand.

The craft of wicker was by no means unknown in the Americas, having arrived with the earliest settlers both as a skill and in the form of lightweight items, such as storage containers, which would have been easier to transport. Wicker cradles were also commonplace—a wicker cradle arrived on the *Mayflower* in 1620. But Wakefield was the first to exploit rattan's considerable advantages in wicker

ABOVE: Portrait of Robert Louis Stevenson (1850–94) painted by John Singer Sargent (1856–1925) and now in the collection of The Taft Museum of Art, Cincinnati. This was the third of Sargent's paintings of Stevenson, painted in 1887 when the author was only thirty-seven years old but already frail. The chair is suggestive of supportive relaxation.

PRECEDING PAGES: Women lounging on the veranda of the Helouhan Hotel, Cairo, Egypt, among a simply stunning collection of rattan furniture. Between 1882 and 1922, Egypt was effectively under British occupation, and hotels played key roles as social centers for a significant expatriate community. Egypt was also a popular travel destination at that time.

ABOVE: Mrs. Sanders and Mr. Russell await refreshments after a day's ride in the desert during the Cairo "Season," 1920s.

One of the most luxurious Egyptian hotels of its day, the Mena House Hotel in Cairo (shown here circa 1935) offered enviable views of the pyramids from the garden. The hotel combined Oriental-style decor with the comforts of an English country house, down to blazing log fires. Naturally, rattan furniture played a starring role.

production and bring it to a broader commercial market. In honor of his achievements, South Reading was renamed Wakefield in 1868.

Heywood Brothers & Company, founded in 1826, chiefly manufactured hardwood furniture. It grew to be a significant rival of Wakefield's once it branched into wicker—the two firms vying with each other to invent new tools and machinery to weave the cane. The concerns eventually merged and pooled their resources in 1897, becoming the Heywood-Wakefield Company. Its "Classic Wicker Furniture" catalog (1898), which advertised the new firm's full range, including end tables, couches, and swings, introduced affordable wicker furniture to a much wider public than ever before. Another great name in American wicker manufacturing is Bielecky Brothers, which was founded by Polish émigrés Andrew and Conrad Bielecky in 1903. The firm is still weaving rattan in their Queens, New York workshop today.

By this time, wicker workshops, or ateliers, had sprung up all over Europe. In France, during the belle époque, Alfred Perret and Ernest Vibert founded their shop in 1872 to provide "natural bamboo

During the late nineteenth and early twentieth centuries, the rattan bistro chair became synonymous with French café society. Maison Drucker, founded in Paris in 1885, was a leading producer, and still makes similar pieces today. A notable feature is colorful patterning in stripes, checkers, zigzags, and chevrons. This evocative shot of the Café de Flore is by renowned Hungarian-American war photographer and photojournalist Robert Capa (1913–54).

furniture and cane seats" for affluent collectors looking to furnish their winter gardens and terraces in an exotic oriental style (similar in design to the furniture of Gabriel Viardot). Selling quietly to clients from their shop on Rue du Quatre-Septembre, they introduced their fantastical vision to a wider audience when they exhibited at the Universal Exhibition of Paris in 1889 to huge acclaim. Cognizant of a growing audience for exotic furnishings and emboldened by two silver medals, Vibert and the son of his founding partner, Alfred, expanded their shop, renaming it La Maison des Bambous, and organized an "exhibition of country furniture and seats for castles and villas." Clients included Claude Debussy, Maurice Ravel, the Duke de Montmorency, Empress Eugénie (for her villa Cyrnos at Cap Martin), George I of Greece (to furnish his winter palace near Athens), and Cornelius Vanderbilt (who commissioned "the great collection of white and gold lacquered flexible rattan seats" for his lobby and greenhouse in New York). Moving its headquarters to Boulevard Hausmann in 1917, La Maison des Bambous continued to sell rattan furniture until it closed its doors in 1994.

The iconic rattan bistro chair, which has become synonymous with French café society, has been in production since 1885, when Louis Drucker founded Maison Drucker in Paris. Designs similar to the original are still made by the brand today.

In the rest of Europe, wicker workshops flourished from the late nineteenth century onward, most notably in Austria and Germany, and to a lesser extent in Holland, Switzerland, and Belgium. The Italian company Bonacina, located north of Milan, opened in 1889 and is still run by the great-grandson of the founder. Employing willow or rattan, or both, some of these were mechanized factories, while others were craft enterprises. The skills passed down through successive generations. Austrian and German wicker furniture, made of willow or cane, along with bentwood pieces, became associated with avant-garde art movements around the turn of the century. Members of the Secession, founded in Vienna in 1897, and

the Deutsche Werkbund, established in Munich in 1907, were heavily influenced by the ideals of William Morris (1834–96) and the Arts and Crafts movement, particularly the emphasis placed on solid construction, fitness for purpose, and the honest use of materials. Among the progressive aims of these artists and designers was to raise the standard of mass-produced goods by forging new links between design schools and commercial firms.

Scandinavia has a rich history of rattan furniture making. The existence today of Sweden's only surviving rattan workshop, Larsson Korgmakare, is, as so often with long-lived rattan workshops, a family story. Founded in 1903 in Stockholm by designer John Larsson, the company is best known for its collaboration with Josef Frank, who designed around a hundred pieces of rattan to be sold through the great Svenskt Tenn design company. Larsson's granddaughter, Erica Larsson, is the fourth generation to weave these enduring designs.

There is plentiful evidence of Russian-made wicker furnishings. In a 1913 World Fair book promoting Russian national crafts, willow from Armenia is specifically mentioned. It is open to conjecture if the rattan furniture that we see in watercolors and photographs of

ABOVE: Villa Mille Fiori—the monumental Beaux-Arts estate in Southampton, Long Island—was commissioned in 1910 by Albert Barnes Boardman and modeled on Rome's Villa Medici. The grandeur of the loggia, with its barrel-vaulted ceiling decorated with Italian murals, Ionic marble columns, and Greek sculptures, is softened by the informal rattan furniture including the Hourglass chair, which was made fashionable after it was exhibited at the Philadelphia Centennial Exhibition of 1876.

OPPOSITE: *Painting of a Woman Reading*, 1880, by William Merritt Chase (1849–1916). The Hourglass rattan chair, as seen opposite, has characteristically wide armrests. Chase, who painted many fashionable women, was a lifelong friend of John Singer Sargent. In 1896, he founded the Chase School of Art in Greenwich Village, renamed the New York School of Art in 1909 and Parsons School of Design in 1936. His studio on Tenth Street in New York City housed various rattan chairs favored by Chase for portrait sittings.

Imperial Russia was made locally, but I very much doubt it. While nothing suggests that rattan was ever imported to Russia as a raw material, rattan furniture first appeared in Russia at the end of the nineteenth century, imported by Prince Golitzin. Because willow grew locally and in abundance, it was favored over the much more expensive non-native rattan, which may explain why weaving in rattan never took hold in Russia.

In India, rattan has been used diversely—in house and boat construction, as roofing material, and furniture production. Ancient texts also cite medicinal uses of rattan. It grows locally and is one of the most valued renewable non-wood forest products.

In Britain, what was generally known as "art cane furniture" was made in significant quantities in the late nineteenth century by a number of companies, some of which specialized exclusively in bamboo, whereas others also used willow, rush, and rattan to make their wickerwork. Established in Nottingham in 1889, Morris, Wilkinson & Co. manufactured "perambulators, mail carts, bassinettes, and invalid carriages," along with utility products

OPPOSITE: Nicholas II (1868–1918), the last czar of Russia, leaning on a high-backed rattan chair. Rattan furniture was first imported from Europe and America to Russia in the middle of the nineteenth century. The czar's brother-in-law and advisor, the Grand Duke Alexander, bought an Abundance rattan chair from the English company Dryad in 1907, soon after the firm was founded.

ABOVE: *A Russian Winter Garden* (1835–38) by Vasily Semyonovich Sadovnikov (1800–79). This is believed to be a view of the Wittgenstein family's winter garden at Pavlino Palace decorated for a ball, with a luxuriant display of ferns, roses, and clematis, along with rattan chairs arranged on the sidelines of a parquet floor cleared for dancing.

such as dress hampers and laundry baskets. Such was the demand for their goods that the firm had to move several times into larger premises. W. T. Ellmore & Son, established in Leicester in 1886, was a similar concern.

In 1904, an article published in the British art publication *The Studio*, extolling the artistic quality of Austrian wicker furniture, helped to popularize these imports in the British market. By this point, the sales of English-made wicker had slumped. Over-elaborate in design and far from robust in construction, it had fallen out of step with the times. All this was soon to change due to the foresight of two friends: Benjamin Fletcher (1868–1951) and Harry Hardy Peach (1874–1936). Both based in Leicester, where Fletcher was the headmaster of Leicester Municipal School of Art (1900–20) and Peach was a bookseller specializing in early printed books, they shared progressive beliefs in design and education. Fletcher introduced Peach to the writings of William Morris and W. R. Lethaby (1857–1931), an architect and educator with whom he regularly corresponded. In accordance with Arts and Crafts principles, Fletcher was particularly keen to strengthen the ties between design education and manufacturing. Peach was also a

social reformer with an interest in politics; later, he wrote to the first Labour prime minister, Ramsay MacDonald, about the dangers of Fascism and the importance of keeping craft skills alive.

In 1905, Fletcher visited Vienna in order to view design developments in the city firsthand. When he returned, he brought back some examples of cane furniture, along with detailed notes on techniques, and enlisted the help of local basket weaver Charles Crampton to experiment with them. The skills of wicker-weaving were well established in Leicester, with willow harvesting long associated with the areas around the rivers Soar and Trent. The following year, Peach was forced to give up bookselling because of his worsening eyesight. Fletcher encouraged him to launch a new venture and set up a company to make cane furniture. Here, they could put their ideas about the importance of design and craftwork into practice.

Dryad Furniture Works opened in February 1907, with Peach as director, Fletcher acting in a design capacity, and Crampton as the principal maker. By the end of the year, the fledgling business occupied a workshop in Leicester and employed four men, and had thirty designs in production.

From the outset, Dryad set itself apart. Using rattan rather than willow or bamboo as the principal raw material, and laying emphasis on soundness of construction, it helped establish cane furniture as fashionable, desirable products for the home. Rather than emulate the rectilinear, geometric Secessionist style, Dryad adopted a different aesthetic more suited to the springy plasticity of rattan, curves that echoed the flowing lines of art nouveau. Their designs exploited rattan's natural resilience, obviating the need for much in the way of additional upholstery. According to Dryad's catalog, the rigidity of the Austrian art cane furniture did not "commend itself to British notions of comfort or fit the homely reserve of British houses."

Thanks in no small part to Peach's canny marketing, the company was successful from the start. Abundance, a 1907 chair design that was well publicized, was purchased in its inaugural year by the Grand Duke Alexander of Russia, brother-in-law of Czar Nicholas II. Along with extensive advertising campaigns, Peach forged links with retail outlets and exhibited Dryad's products at every available opportunity. To reach the widest possible market, there was also a mail-order side to the business and a comprehensive catalog to go along with it. Product names were chosen to evoke nostalgia; advertising copy stressed sound workmanship: "a strong sensible log basket," "a well-made cane chair is cheaper and more convenient that an upholstered one." Before long, the company had established a reputation for superbly made original designs.

The firm rapidly grew from strength to strength, employing fifty men in 1911, one hundred in 1913, and doubling its workforce again the year after. By 1914, Dryad was exporting its wares all over the world and had retail outlets in New York and Chicago, where it

ABOVE: At the time of its ill-fated maiden voyage in 1912, the British passenger liner RMS *Titanic* was the largest ship afloat. Sumptuously furnished and decorated, it was the latest in seaborne comfort. Here, first-class passengers are taking tea.

ABOVE: Portable, lightweight, and robust, rattan chairs, tables, and loungers made perfect shipboard furnishings. Czar Nicholas II and Czarina Alexandra Fyodorovna are pictured relaxing on the imperial yacht *Standart* with Dryad-designed furniture. When the yacht came into service in 1896, it was the largest royal yacht in the world and was decorated as a floating palace. During the Second World War, it played a role in the defense of Leningrad.

LEFT: Relaxing on white-painted rattan chairs, a group of friends take the sea air aboard a yacht in 1938.

OPPOSITE: Venezuelan socialite Mrs. Herrera and Count Rudi Crespi, photographed by Henry Clarke for *Vogue*, relax on board a cruise ship, 1955. Count Crespi helped to promote Italian fashion in the United States.

Aïn Kassimou is a villa in Marrakech originally built in the nineteenth century for Olga Tolstoy and later owned by Marella Agnelli. This terrace, shaded by a split-bamboo pergola and planted with bougainvillea, immediately adjoined Agnelli's bedroom and is furnished with her beloved wicker. The gardens were designed by Madison Cox.

rivaled the dominance of the Heywood-Wakefield Company. One of the firm's most significant commissions came when it secured the contract to supply rattan chairs and tables for the lounge areas on the RMS *Titanic*, notably for the Café Parisien, which was decorated to suggest a sidewalk café. By this time, Dryad's business had expanded so much it was forced to move to larger premises.

During the First World War, while many of Dryad's workforce joined up or were conscripted, the firm shifted its production to the making of stretchers for wounded soldiers, baskets for observation balloons, and wickerwork shell and ammunition casings. The civic-minded Peach donated offcuts of cane to a local hospital so that recuperating soldiers could engage in the therapeutic craft of basket weaving.

The firm was also one of several contracted by the Aircraft Supplies Co. Ltd. to make rattan pilot seats for Sopwith Camels, the leading British fighter plane of the Royal Flying Corps (forerunner of the RAF), thousands of which were manufactured during the war. In a recent blog on the role basketry played in the First World War, Professor Owen Davies of the University of Hertfordshire quotes a 1916 editorial from the magazine *The Aeroplane*: "It has been thought inadvisable to have one of the famous Dryad chairs in the editorial offices of *The Aeroplane*, lest visitors might be tempted to

ABOVE: Artists Michael Lambert Tree (1921–99) and Lucian Freud (1922–2011) photographed by Cecil Beaton under the portico at Mereworth Castle in Kent. Designed in the 1720s by Colen Campbell as a near-replica of Palladio's Villa Rotunda, Mereworth was, at the time of this photograph, the home of Tree (the son of politician Ronald Tree and Nancy Lancaster) and his wife, Lady Anne Cavendish.

ABOVE: Rattan has a long history of use as nursery furniture and accessories—from bassinets and baby carriages to cradles and nursing chairs. A wicker cradle arrived on the Mayflower with the early settlers.

stay too long to the detriment of the daily routine." The Sopwith Camel seats, Davies notes, cost around six shillings and three pence each, which represented excellent value for money compared to fully upholstered seats.

Light, flexible, and strong, rattan seating had been employed in airplanes from 1912 onward to reduce weight and absorb inflight stresses. Dryad would continue to make basketwork airplane seats after the war for commercial aircraft. When Charles Lindbergh made his pioneering solo flight across the Atlantic in 1927, his seat in *Spirit of St. Louis* was made of rattan. The plane is now in the Smithsonian's National Air and Space Museum in Washington, DC.

Between the wars, rattan furniture became a familiar sight not only in private gardens and conservatories but also on board ocean liners and steamers, and on private yachts, in sanatoriums,

ABOVE: Italian actress Claudia Cardinale (b. 1938) on the set of the epic 1963 film *Il Gattopardo* (The Leopard), based on Giuseppe Tomasi di Lampedusa's novel of the same title.

clubs, cafés, tearooms, hotel lounges, palm courts, and winter gardens. Dryad's catalogs, featuring designs named Travellers' Joy and Sluggard's Lure, reinforced the associations with travel and recreation. As well as chairs, tables, and settees, there was also a plethora of rattan accessories on offer, ranging from tiered cake stands to garden trugs, many of which were shown at the Chelsea Flower Show in 1937.

By this point, other companies had begun to wake up to the commercial potential of rattan furniture. At home, Dryad's principal competitor, Ellmore, also based in Leicester, spruced up its act by adopting similar design and marketing strategies, until it closed in 1926, while Angraves, founded in 1912 in Thurmaston, Leicester, would be still trading nearly a century later, when it was the last surviving producer of cane furniture in Britain.

ABOVE: A woman reclines on a rattan lounger in a conservatory designed by Lord & Burnham, founded in 1849 and soon to become one of the leading American manufacturers of conservatories and greenhouses.

OPPOSITE: Villa Agnelli, the eighteenth-century estate at Villar Perosa at the foot of the Italian Alps in Piedmont, was where Marella Agnelli began to develop her distinctive style. The loggia on the *piano nobile*, overlooking gardens created by the landscape designer Russell Page, is furnished with antique rattan, chosen with the help of Stéphane Boudin, the head of Paris-based decorating firm Maison Jansen.

Nothing less than an exotic haven, Mr. Kenneth's beauty salon, which opened in New York in 1963, was decorated by Billy Baldwin, who also created fabulous interiors for Diana Vreeland and Babe Paley, among many others. Inspired by the Royal Pavilion at Brighton, layered with pattern and color, it was the place to be seen and to be pampered. Rattan chairs with leopard-print cushions added to the theater of the manicure and hairdryer stations with their fabric-lined walls and tented ceilings. Mr. Kenneth, no less than Baldwin, had an extraordinary clientele: he was hairdresser to both Jacqueline Kennedy Onassis and Marilyn Monroe.

There was also rivalry from Lloyd Loom, which produced mass-market furniture and storage pieces using paper-wrapped wire to emulate wicker. Its sheet construction ensured the furniture was less time-consuming to produce, and therefore traditional hand-woven rattan could not begin to compete in terms of cost. While the technique was invented and patented by an American, Marshall B. Lloyd, who set up a plant in Menominee, Michigan, Lloyd Loom was also manufactured in Britain, after the British rights were sold in 1921 to W. Lusty & Sons, a firm based in Bromley-by-Bow in London's East End. Between the wars, Lloyd Loom furniture became exceptionally popular on both sides of the Atlantic: some ten million pieces were sold up to 1940. Whether American- or British-made, this so-called wicker furniture was a familiar sight not only in the home but also wherever rattan itself was prevalent—in lounges and tearooms, as well as on board ships.

After the Second World War, rattan lost ground in the mass market to synthetic materials coming into widespread use, most notably various types of plastic. Yet the seeds of rattan's eventual comeback were already being planted as a new generation of mid-century modern designers discovered its potential to create expressive, sculptural forms. At the same time, a number of highly influential tastemakers—from Marella Agnelli to Bunny Mellon—sought out unpretentious rattan furniture and accessories as a foil for the grandeur of their interiors, transforming humble wicker into a signifier of old-school glamour.

Japan's longest-surviving rattan business, Yamakawa Rattan, founded in 1952 by Hichiro Yamakawa in Tokyo, has a poignant story. It was started in Yamakawa's backyard as a therapeutic outlet for the creativity of his two hearing-impaired sons. A third son studied design in order to further grow and promote the family business. Yamakawa Rattan, now producing their furniture in their own Indonesian workshops, was the first Japanese company to have one of its designs selected for the permanent collection of the Museum of Modern Art (MoMA) in New York in 1964.

ABOVE: Tony Duquette (1914–99) was a virtuoso design talent who created movie sets for Vincente Minnelli and jewelry for the Duchess of Windsor, along with many bravura interiors. The teahouse at his ranch, Sortilegium, in Malibu's Santa Monica Mountains confirms his reputation as a "maximalist icon." Elsie de Wolfe was his mentor and introduced him to her Hollywood circle of friends.

OPPOSITE: American socialite Pat Buckley, wife of conservative commentator William F. Buckley Jr., as photographed by Ernst Beadle for *Vogue*. The sunroom of her home in Stamford, Connecticut, designed by Tom Fleming of Irvine and Fleming, had French doors that led onto a terrace with rattan chairs, 1975.

Rattan's renewed popularity in the 1960s and '70s coincided with a fascination for the exotic, born on the hippie trail, and the nostalgic resurrection of various period styles—from art deco to Victoriana. However, due to its association with those living alternative lifestyles, rattan fell from favor once again, victim to the hectic turnover of fashion trends. After another period of eclipse, the present-day rattan revival is more design-driven—the eco-friendliness and sustainability of the material only adding to rattan's desirability.

With a pedigree stretching back thousands of years, rattan is a great survivor. Thanks to its great design potential and versatility, its natural origins and romantic associations, it is simply too extraordinary a material not to be.

OPPOSITE: *Three Women Sewing in a Garden* (1923) by French post-Impressionist painter Henri Lebasque (1865–1937). Lebasque's travels in the south of France had a profound effect on his color palette.

ABOVE: Rattan chairs from the 1950s flank a rattan marquetry wardrobe in an attic bedroom at Hôtel Drujon—the Provençal home of Anthony Watson and Benoit Rauzy, founders of Atelier Vime, a design studio and workshop based in Vallabrègues, Provence.

Great Designs

GREAT DESIGNS

Rattan's essential fluidity as a material allows for the expression of a wide range of styles. Woven into a tight mesh or open and airy, generously curved or severely rectilinear, it has provided endless possibilities for designers over the years.

On occasion, rattan has played a reticent role—simply one of any number of materials employed to execute a design. Early on, for example, it was adopted as a lighter, cleaner alternative to upholstery for chairs and sofas—a function it continued to perform in early modernist designs. As familiarity with the material grew during the nineteenth century, it was also used to create furniture that followed classic forms: dining, arm, and rocking chairs and tea tables and sofas. Most intriguingly, however, has been its fashioning into sculptural, organic designs that make the most of its malleability: furniture that could only have been made in rattan.

While nineteenth-century rattan furniture was never attributed to a specific designer, there were recognizable types. Wicker photographer's chairs, for example, were common studio props in the late nineteenth century. Often asymmetrical and generally highly ornate, they served as intriguing focal points around which to arrange groups posing for formal portraits. Theme or "motif" wicker was even more elaborate, incorporating pictorial representations—such as tennis rackets, flags, or sailing ships— in the back panels of chairs or sofas. In general, however, rattan furniture was produced in the prevailing style of its era, with the intricate designs of High Victoriana giving way to simpler forms by the turn of the century. Mission wicker was typically framed in straight lines, whereas so-called Bay Harbor–style wicker, made in willow or rattan, formed shapes framing diamond-patterned latticing. In "stick" wicker, the willow or rattan was not woven;

Orangery chair, Napoleon III, France, circa 1850.

Wakefield Rattan Company, USA, circa 1890.

Hans Vollmer for Prag-Rudniker, Vienna Secession, Austria, circa 1900.

Ludwig Mies van der Rohe, MR side chair for Knoll, Germany, 1927.

Henry van de Velde, Germany, 1906–08.

Arne Jacobsen for Sika, Paris chair, Denmark, 1920s.

Erich Dieckmann, Bauhaus, Germany, 1920s.

Jean-Michel Frank for Ecart International, France, 1930s.

Paul Frankl, Pretzel chair, USA, circa 1934.

PAGE 80: Eureka hanging chair designed by Giovanni Travasa for Bonacina in 1958.

PAGE 81: The Hanging Egg chair designed by Nanna and Jørgen Ditzel for Sika in 1959 has become a Danish design icon. Here, it is modeled by one of their daughters.

OPPOSITE: *By the Seashore*, 1883, by French artist Pierre-Auguste Renoir (1841–1919). The background is believed to depict Guernsey in the Channel Islands, which Renoir visited in 1883.

ABOVE: The P3 lounge chair was designed by Tito Agnoli (1931–2012) and produced by Bonacina in 1964. Agnoli originally studied painting, then went to work as an assistant to Gio Ponti. He specialized in furniture, lighting, and industrial design. This recliner features rattan woven around a tubular steel framework. Its ergonomic shape is very comfortable to sit in.

instead, the framework was formed of parallel vertical reeds or stakes. Hourglass chairs in rattan were first shown in America at the 1876 Centennial Exposition in Philadelphia as part of the Chinese Imperial Maritime Customs Collection.

One of the earliest named designs is the archetypal Peacock chair. Also known as the Manila or Philippine chair, it is thought to have originated in the late nineteenth century, when inmates, possibly of Bilibid Prison in Manila, were set the task of weaving household furnishings out of rattan. At this time, no single name was associated with the design of this chair, which was to achieve iconic status. It appears to have first arrived in the United States around 1915.

With its high, curved back forming a flattering halo-like frame for the face and exotic hourglass-shaped base, it was not long before the Peacock chair became widely adopted as an exotic place to pose for a photograph. As the century progressed, this throne-like seat appeared in countless publicity shots of celebrities, movie stars, and musicians.

In 1967, the Peacock chair gained a new layer of meaning when Huey Newton, the founder of the Black Panther movement, was pictured sitting in one, holding a rifle in one hand, a spear in the

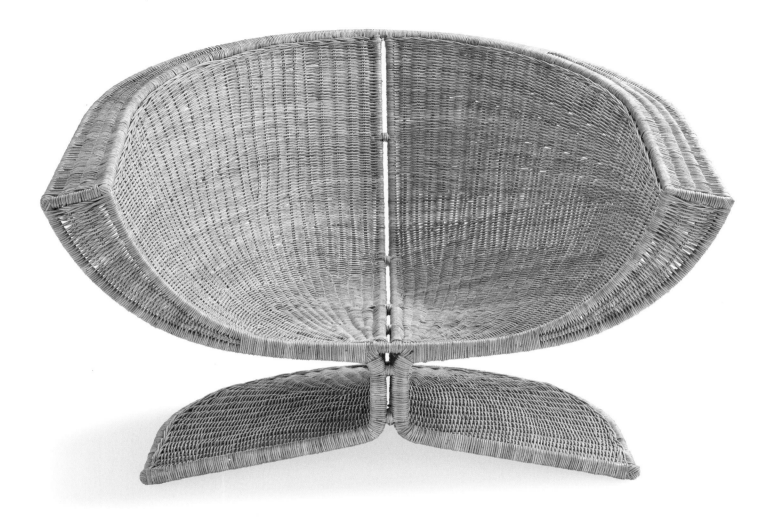

other, and surrounded by African tribal masks, a zebra rug covering the floor. Despite the chair's Southeast Asian, rather than African, origins, this strong image transformed the design into a lasting symbol of black power. When Newton was in prison, the chair was occasionally displayed unoccupied at meetings as a stand-in for his presence.

An association of a rather different kind came about in 1974 when Sylvia Kristel, star of the French soft porn film *Emmanuelle*, posed topless in a Peacock chair for the movie poster. By this point, rattan was already somewhat on the wane in glamorous interiors. The risqué overtones did little to stem its decline.

Arguably, rattan first received serious attention when various members of the Secession, established in Vienna in 1897, and the Deutsche Werkbund, founded in Munich in 1907, designed furniture using the material. These turn-of-the-century avant-garde artists, designers, and architects strongly influenced by the Arts and Crafts movement, were dedicated to dissolving the boundaries between fine art and craft and to forge new links with industry. Like William Morris half a century before, they were dismayed at the poor quality of the goods being produced by factories. Unlike Morris, however, who rejected mechanization and devoted his life to the revival

ABOVE: Designed by Miller Yee Fong in 1968, and manufactured by Tropi-Cal, the Lotus chair epitomizes the sophisticated yet casual Californian lifestyle. The rusticity of the material and organic form are married to an elegant modernity.

FOLLOWING PAGES: Barbour's *Woman Reading* (circa 1910) shows a fashionable young woman reclining on a rattan lounger. Sterling and Francine Clark Art Institute, Williamstown, Massachusetts.

Franco Albini for Bonacina, Italy, circa 1950s.

Mathieu Matégot, Kimono chair, France, 1954.

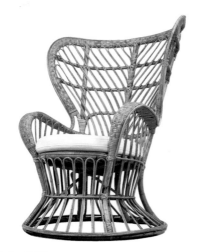

Italy, 1950s.

Louis Sognot, France, circa 1955.

Jean Royère, France, 1950s.

Jacques Adnet, France, 1950s.

Janine Abraham and Dirk Jan Rol, Lemon chair, France, 1957.

Karl Fostel Sr., Austria, 1950s.

Marcel Breuer for Thonet, S35 chair, Germany, 1930s.

OPPOSITE: Toshio Yano for Yamakawa Rattan, Kani ("crab") chair, Japan, 1960s.

In 1954, Serge Obolensky bought the opulent Ambassador Hotel on Park Avenue, New York City, and invited Cecil Beaton to decorate a suite on the thirteenth floor. Beaton created a "bogus Japanese" interior with a geometric print decorating the walls, ceiling, and screens, and an emerald-green carpet and crimson silk tablecloth. The contemporary atmosphere was transformed by the addition of intricate white-painted Edwardian rattan furniture, bought from the glamorous spa resort, the Grand Union Hotel, at Saratoga Springs.

of traditional craft skills, these precursors of modernism sought to integrate design more fully within the production process; their radical ideas helped to pave the way for the Bauhaus. Wicker made of cane or willow, along with bentwood, were some of the more humble materials with which they experimented.

Gustav Funke, director of the Imperial School, Vienna, created both individual items of wicker furniture and patterns to be incorporated within wicker pieces. Hans Vollmer (1897–1946) served as a furniture designer for the Prag-Rudniker Korbwaren-Fabrikation (or Basketwork Factory), as did Koloman Moser (1868–1918), who produced geometric chairs with checkerboard weaves for the 1903 Klimt exhibition at the Secession building. Prag-Rudniker, first registered in Prague in 1886, grew rapidly until it could boast of being the largest wickerwork company in Europe, employing 2,500 workers in factories in Budapest, Prague, Rudnik (Poland), and Vienna, and exporting worldwide.

Similarly, Henry van de Velde (1863–1957), Peter Behrens (1868–1940), and Richard Riemerschmid (1868–1957) all produced designs for cane and wicker furniture in the art nouveau style with Riemerschmid forming a creative partnership with the Dresden furniture company Theodor Reimann. Many of these designs were exhibited and others widely publicized. Typically, they were rectilinear, often having square openings within the weave.

Josef Hoffmann (1870–1956), one of the founding members of the Secession, who went on to cofound the Wiener Werkstätte (Vienna Workshops) in 1903, was a prolific designer in many fields: glass, textiles, silver, metalwork, furniture, and architecture. He was also an influential teacher. Gridded geometric forms characterize much of his work. In the 1920s, he and Josef Frank (1885–1967) created the Model 811 chair. Also known as the Prague chair, it had an elegantly curved bentwood frame and arms in birch with a tightly woven cane seat and back. A variant on the ubiquitous Thonet bentwood

café chair, which sold in the millions, this model was later manufactured by the same company.

Frank went on to design many items of rattan furniture for the Swedish company Svenskt Tenn, along with a range of boldly colored textiles celebrating flora and fauna. In the 1930s, Frank emigrated from Vienna to Stockholm with his Swedish wife to escape the growing menace of anti-Semitism. Ten years after Estrid Ericson established Svenskt Tenn in Stockholm in 1924, she asked Frank to design for her. His furniture, sitting somewhat outside contemporary trends, was comfortable, ergonomically scaled, and easy to live with. Frank's rattan designs, such as his 311 sofa and armchair (1930s) and 1165 and 1184 chairs (1940s), typically shared a lightness with their airy frameworks and slender, rounded forms.

Rattan's versatility had not escaped the attention of pioneering modernist designers. Ludwig Mies van der Rohe (1886–1969) and Marcel Breuer (1902–81) eschewed bentwood for the more radical machine aesthetic of tubular steel, taking inspiration from bicycle frames and other modern mass-produced products. Rattan, in the form of caned seats and backs, may have played a supplementary role in many of their iconic chair designs, but it contributed an important visual lightness. Mies's MR20 cantilever chair (1927) was not the first of its type, but its generous curves give it the sculptural quality that has deservedly afforded it enduring appeal. Breuer's cantilever design of 1928 has been produced by Thonet since 1930 and remains a familiar sight in both office and domestic settings. Similarly, an early cantilever chair by the Danish functionalist designer Mogens Lassen (1901–87) bears a striking resemblance to Mies's version, although the rattan seat is more prominent—and is not unlike the pilot seats that were produced for the airplanes of the day. The German designer Erich Dieckmann (1896–1944), who was apprenticed at the Bauhaus, the radical art and design school founded in 1919 by Walter

Viggo Boesen for Sika, Fox chair, Denmark, 1936.

Illum Wikkelso, Ring chair no. 23, Denmark, 1950s.

Aksel Bender Madsen and Ejner Larsen for Willy Beck, Metropolitan chair, Denmark, 1950s.

OPPOSITE: Armchairs designed by Peter Hvidt and Orla Mølgaard-Nielsen for Søborg, Denmark, 1950s.

ABOVE: Austrian-born Paul Frankl helped to popularize art deco in the United States. In the 1940s, his fascination with Chinese and Japanese art led him to design rattan pieces that epitomized the informal California lifestyle.

Hans Wegner for Carl Hansen & Søn, CH27, Denmark, 1950s.

Giovanni Travasa for Bonacina, Palla chair, Italy, 1966.

René-Jean Caillette for Charron, armchair prototype, France, 1962.

Giovanni Travasa for Bonacina, Eva chair, Italy, 1965.

Tom Dixon for Capellini, S-Chair, UK, 1988.

Janine Abraham and Dirk Jan Rol, France, 1960s.

Giuseppe Raboni for Bonacina, SuperElastica, Italy, 2005.

Mats Theselius for IKEA, Sweden, early 2000s.

Soane Britain, Venus chair, UK, 2010.

OPPOSITE: The dining room in Villa Mabrouka, Tangier, was designed by Jacques Grange for Pierre Bergé and Yves Saint Laurent. It has nineteenth-century lamps from Madeleine Castaing's shop in Paris as well as rattan chairs, manufactured by McGuire, echoing the walls lined in bamboo matting.

ABOVE: Lounge chair designed by Michel Buffet in the 1950s, pictured here at Galerie Chenel in Paris.

PAGE 98: Philanthropist, socialite, and author Brooke Astor (1902–2007) standing behind a wicker chair with three of her dogs. A features editor at *House & Garden* during the 1940s, Astor employed Ruby Ross Wood and Billy Baldwin to decorate the New York apartment she shared with her second husband, Charles Henry Marshall. Photograph by Horst P. Horst for *Vogue*, 1962.

PAGE 99: The kitchen at the Hôtel Drujon in Vallabrègues, Provence, with the Gabriel rattan pendant light and The Eye placemats, both by Atelier Vime design studio and workshop. The rattan dining chairs were designed by Adrien Audoux and Frida Minet in the 1960s and made in France.

Gropius in Weimar, also combined rattan with tubular steel in his own cantilever chair. Later, he went on to employ the material more extensively in his rigorously geometric designs for the manufacturer Gelenka, generally in the form of cane seats and backs.

Early modernists such as Mies, Breuer, and Le Corbusier (1887–1965) adhered to a strict functionalism in the designs of their furniture, buildings, and interiors. Although highly influential, their work did not achieve much commercial success until decades later. Far more popular during the 1920s and 1930s was art deco, a style that blended a diverse range of influences: the vibrant colors and exoticism of the Ballets Russes, skyscrapers, recent archeological discoveries in Egypt, and stepped ziggurat forms, to name but a few. Streamlining, the new language of industrial design, was also evident in art deco's boldly delineated geometric shapes.

The Paris chair (1925) by Arne Jacobsen (1902–71) emphasizes rattan's suitability for the new style. Designed while Jacobsen was still a student, the chair won a silver medal at the 1925 Exposition Internationale des Arts Décoratifs et Industriels Modernes in Paris, but was not put into production until after the Second World War. With an undulating reclining seat supported by side panels shaped like half-wheels, the entire piece is animated by an almost kinetic sense of movement.

Designed over a decade later, Jacobsen's Charlottenborg chair, two-seater sofa, and side table (1936) display a similar art deco aesthetic. Bent rattan is used to create the generous curves of the frames and ladder-like back rests. Dating from the same year is the Fox chair by Viggo Boesen (1907–85), a Danish designer who valued rattan for its strength and durability; the design was awarded a prize by the Danish Guild of Wickermakers.

RIGHT, FROM TOP TO BOTTOM:

Dennis Abalos for Feelgood Designs, Snug chair, Australia, 2011.

Franca Helg for Bonacina, Primavera chair, Italy, 1967.

Mathieu Matégot, Ferotin chair, France, 1952.

OPPOSITE: Overhead view of Franco Albini's Margherita chairs for Bonacina. This design won an award at the Milan Triennale in 1951.

ABOVE: Arne Jacobsen is pictured here in his iconic Paris chair with Flemming Lassen. In 1929, the pair won a Danish Architects Association competition for designing the "House of the Future."

French interior designer Jean-Michel Frank (1895–1941) was known for his use of luxurious art deco materials such as mica and shagreen, a glittering client list that included Nelson Rockefeller and Salvador Dalí, and his refined furniture designs, so pared-back as to be almost minimal. An example is the Parsons table, which he developed in the 1930s in association with the Paris branch of the famous New York design school. For Ecart, Frank also produced a range of rattan furniture, which shared the same simplicity of form.

LEFT: At Yves Saint Laurent and Pierre Bergé's Villa Mabrouka, this bedroom was decorated with walls lined in woven rattan inspired by Bergé's similar bedroom at his nearby Villa Léon l'Africain.

Austrian-born Paul Frankl (1886–1958) was another designer who helped to popularize art deco. When he first arrived in New York as a young émigré, he was dazzled by the confident energy expressed by the city's skyline. Trained as an architect in Vienna and Berlin, where modernism had its beginnings, he made it his mission to introduce the same spirit into American furniture design. His early designs, the Skyscraper furniture range (1926), echoed the angular stepped forms of the buildings he could see around him. These were sold through his recently opened showroom; although expensive, they attracted a great deal of publicity.

In 1934, Frankl moved to Los Angeles, where he opened a gallery in Beverly Hills, catering to Hollywood clients such as Fred Astaire, Cary Grant, Katharine Hepburn, and Alfred Hitchcock. In the relaxed Californian milieu, his furniture became more expansive and organic in form. Inspired by his fascination with Chinese and Japanese

ABOVE: When Jacques Grange first visited Comporta, on the remote west coast of Portugal in the late 1980s, "it was like the Hamptons a hundred years ago." Subsequently, Grange and his partner, Pierre Passebon, chose to build a holiday home here, decorating it in a rustic style. It incorporates many woven plant materials, including rattan chairs and tabletops, mixed with graphic African textiles and unfinished timber walls, creating a deeply relaxed and unpretentious atmosphere.

When Harald and Jeanette Mix decided to redecorate their early twentieth-century redbrick house in Stockholm, they turned to London-based designer Ilse Crawford, who had so cleverly designed their beautiful hotel, Ett Hem, a few years earlier. The rattan armchairs designed by Arne Jacobsen soften the grandeur of the room.

art, rattan was the obvious material from which to fashion his entirely novel Pretzel chairs and sofas (1940–49), with their curvaceous frames made of six to nine strands of bent rattan. He also designed ottomans and stepped end tables in a similar style. Frankl was one of the first designers to mix rattan with upholstered furniture and to introduce it into areas of the home, such as dining rooms and living rooms, where it had not commonly been seen before. In this, he was influenced by the more informal Californian lifestyle, which blurred the boundaries between indoors and outdoors.

By mid-century, modernism had entered a second phase. After the war, a new generation of designers in Scandinavia, Italy, France, and the United States rediscovered a more human, expressive dimension, combining clean modern lines with organic forms, drawing on both artificial and natural materials. The spirit was optimistic and forward-looking. With this more popular wave of modernism, rattan was given a new lease on life.

Scandinavian modern design burst onto the international scene in the late 1940s, becoming increasingly desirable as leading stores such as Bonniers began selling these products across the country. Danish modern, as it was popularly known in the United

States, first came to the attention of the American design community when Edgar Kaufmann Jr. chose Danish pieces to furnish Fallingwater, that landmark of twentieth-century architecture Frank Lloyd Wright had built for Kaufmann's father, a wealthy Pittsburgh businessman. Kaufmann Jr., a noted aesthete, played a prominent role at New York's MoMA, and his endorsement validated the museum's founding aspiration to be "the greatest museum of modern art in the word."

Relatively affordable, easy to live with, and scaled to suit smaller postwar houses and apartments, Danish modern was largely crafted from natural materials and represented an evolutionary modernism that elevated human comfort. While a signature material was teak, rattan was favored in many classic Scandinavian designs, sometimes relatively unobtrusively in the form of woven seats and backs, sometimes more emphatically. Poul Kjaerholm's PK22 chair (1955) and PK80 daybed (1957) produced by Sika exemplify this, with the original leather seat material being replaced by woven rattan as part of their Icons range. Sika was founded during the war, at a time when raw materials were virtually unobtainable; their earliest products were wicker baskets made of reeds and waste straw left over after harvest.

ABOVE: Neighboring the Kyoto Imperial Palace, Nazuna Kyoto Gosho is a small *ryokan* incorporating two traditional Kyoto-style town houses. The focal point of this bedroom is a rattan armchair designed by Isamu Kenmochi for Yamakawa in 1960.

OPPOSITE: A pair of Relation sofas, with their woven rattan seats, designed by Hiroomi Tahara for Yamakawa. The fine legs, made of metal but designed to look like a single piece of rattan, echo the bamboo trunks in the background.

One of the most prolific Danish modern designers was Hans Wegner (1914–2007). Tireless in his pursuit of perfection, Wegner's work was instrumental in bringing the style to prominence in the United States. For him, that ideal could be found in simplicity; the best of his designs are essays in pure form. One such example is the Round chair (1949), also known as PP501, or simply "The Chair." Proclaimed "the world's most beautiful chair" when it appeared on the cover of the American magazine *Interiors* in 1950, it was thrust into the limelight when it was chosen by CBS as seating for the first-ever televised presidential debate between John F. Kennedy and Richard Nixon in 1960.

Like many of Wegner's designs, the chair incorporated rattan elements in the form of a woven cane seat and cane wrapping around the back rail. The cane wrapping was originally intended to disguise the joints in the rail where the back piece met the arms, and thus

give the illusion of a single continuous rail. Later, when Wegner perfected the joint, the rattan wrapping was omitted. Some versions of the chair substituted paper cord for rattan. A more extensive use of rattan is evident in the PP512 folding chair (1949). This low-slung lounge chair has a geometric oak frame and a caned seat and back. Wegner also employed rattan more incidentally to create gridded mesh panels in sideboards and cabinets, or as magazine shelves in coffee tables.

Simultaneously, Egon Eiermann (1904–70), one of Germany's most important postwar architects and a pioneering furniture designer, was innovating with rattan. His study of rattan craftsmanship inspired him to allow the process to dictate the form, celebrating the material's sculptural versatility, exemplified by his design of the E10 and E14 chair and stool.

Many Danish designers, including Arne Jacobsen, Viggo Boesen (1907–85), Nanna Ditzel (1923–2005), and Kay Bojesen (1886–1958), originally experimented with rattan in collaboration with Robert Wengler (1825–1902). German-born Wengler, regarded as a pioneer of rattan production, had set up his Copenhagen firm around the beginning of the twentieth century. In 1914, the company had been commissioned by King Christian X to execute a large order of wicker furniture for the royal household.

The Finnish architect and designer Alvar Aalto (1898–1976), in common with many of his Scandinavian Modern contemporaries, had a great respect for materials and technical experimentation. He is recognized as being the first designer who popularized the cantilever in bent plywood. The lightweight atmosphere of his bentwood Armchair 45 (1947) is enhanced when paired with rattan as opposed to the more common linen and leather used for upholstery.

Nanna Ditzel made expressive use of the material, placing it center stage. In her Hanging Egg chair (1957), an evocative ovoid form suspended from a chain, the wickerwork providing a fluid, tactile enclosure. Far from being incidental to the design, rattan is the whole point of it. Other Ditzel creations in rattan include the Nanny rocking chair (1969), the Madame lounge chair and the Chill

Sophia Bush's 1950s modernist house in the Hollywood Hills saw Bush collaborate with interior designer Jake Alexander Arnold. Vintage rattan chairs from County Ltd. sit harmoniously with a Paul Rusconi artwork and Eames screen.

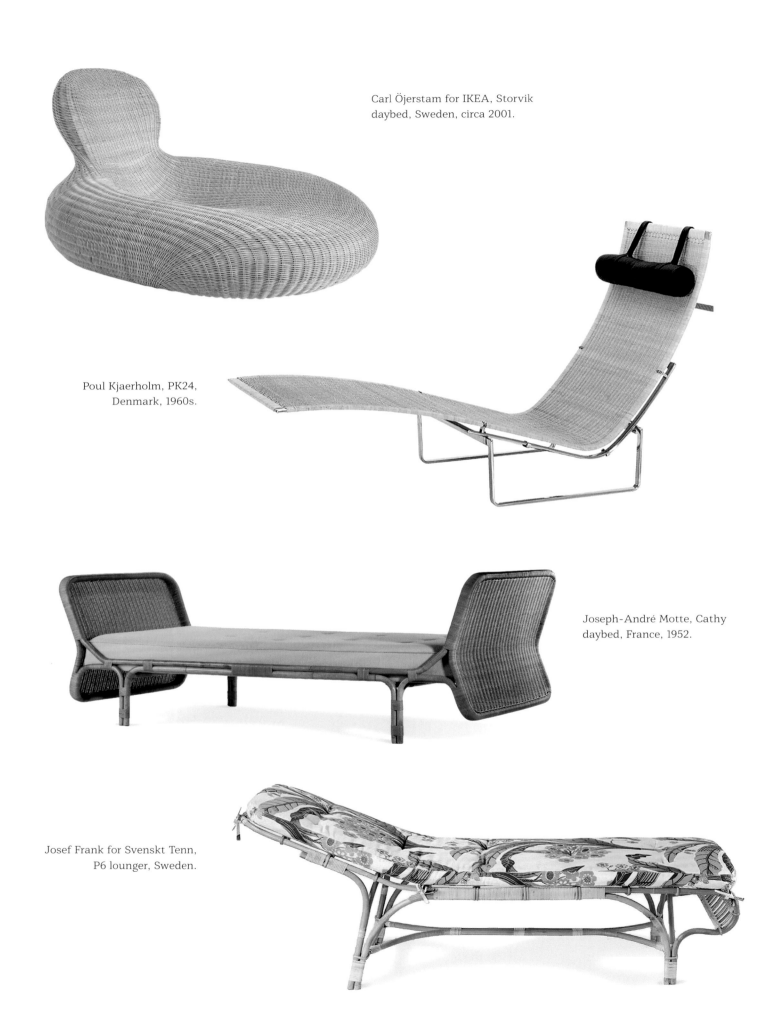

Carl Öjerstam for IKEA, Storvik daybed, Sweden, circa 2001.

Poul Kjaerholm, PK24, Denmark, 1960s.

Joseph-André Motte, Cathy daybed, France, 1952.

Josef Frank for Svenskt Tenn, P6 lounger, Sweden.

lounge chair and footstool (1961). Rana, a three-legged rattan chair, dramatically integrates the shell with the frame.

Lesser known than their Scandinavian counterparts, and still under-recognized today, were a number of postwar French designers who worked in rattan. The earliest of this group, Louis Sognot (1892–1970), had been a noted designer in the art deco style, much of whose work was in metal. During the 1930s, however, he increasingly turned to rattan as a more affordable material. Postwar, his furniture, which

included luxurious *bateaux lits*, dressing tables, recliners, chairs, and sideboards, were typically produced in rattan and wood. Most took more traditional forms than his previous art deco designs, some borne on minimal frames of stick wicker.

Both Roger Landault (1919–83) and Jean Royère (1902–81), the latter in collaboration with Maison Gouffé, designed extensively in rattan during the 1950s and '60s. Landault's work was typically rather skeletal in form with minimal weaving, while Royère combined open diamond-shaped latticing with more densely woven elements. His elegant high-backed chairs with a skirted effect around the seat are reminiscent of drapery.

The French modernist René-Jean Caillette (1919–2005), whose furniture was designed for mass production, often worked in new materials such as plywood, plastic, and aluminum. His molded-plywood Diamond chair (1958) is a contemporary French classic. Rattan was another material that featured in his chair designs, chiefly in the form of caned seating supported by clean-lined metal frameworks.

Joseph-André Motte (1925–2013), who had been a student of Sognot's, was well known for his large-scale public projects. While he was fascinated by the design potential of plastic, he also used rattan in a number of designs—in part because it offered the same malleability.

The producer of Motte's rattan pieces was Edition Rougier, a Paris-based atelier. Edition Rougier also made much of the rattan designed by husband-and-wife creative partnership of Janine Abraham (1929–2005) and Dutch-born Dirk Jan Rol (b. 1929), whose practice encompassed furniture design, interiors, and architecture. Rol, who had originally trained as a cabinetmaker in the Netherlands and later as an interior designer and architect in Paris, met Abraham in 1955 when she was already attracting attention as a rising young designer. After they married and set up their design consultancy, Abraham & Rol, in 1957, all their work was jointly credited. Abraham's signature, however, could be seen in the inventive fluidity of their furniture designs, while Rol contributed more of an architectonic quality.

OPPOSITE: Susanna Agnelli, Countess Rattazzi (1922–2009), with her daughter Delfina Rattazzi at home in Santa Liberata, near the Italian coastal town of Porto Ercole, in August 1980. Agnelli was an Italian politician and writer. Her autobiography, *Vestivamo alla marinara* (We Always Wore Sailor Suits), was a bestseller in Italy.

ABOVE: Designer David Netto decorated this Case Study house with, among other things, rattan chaises from IKEA. "I love chaises contoured like a wave, without any straight lines—you can see how much sensuality the shape and material bring to the somewhat strict modernist backdrop of the house. I can still remember how good it felt to sit in them."

OPPOSITE: There is rhythmic beauty to the iconic Primavera table, designed by Italian architect Franca Helg for Bonacina in 1967.

A range of rattan seats designed for Rougier was exhibited in 1956 at the Société des Artistes Décorateurs (SAD). Soleil, a circular seat with a springy form, won a Gold Medal at the World's Fair in Brussels in 1958, and was one of the pieces chosen to furnish Shah Mohammad Reza Pahlavi's palace in Tehran.

Influenced by traditional Japanese houses and interiors, and by contemporary American architecture, Abraham and Rol's furniture married clean lines with expressive elements, a role for which rattan is particularly well suited. Designs such as the easy chair Citron (1957) and the AR65 table lamp, which resembles a space rocket poised for liftoff, make the most of rattan's potential to create evocative patterns of light and shade when fashioned into sculptural frameworks—the shadow images, which shift according to the angle of the sun, animate each piece with immense personality. Often the curvilinear rattan forms were paired with more linear metal elements, such as in the low-slung Bourboule chair of 1954, where a slipper seat made of rattan is supported by spindly metal legs.

A similar aesthetic can be found in the work of Dutch designer Dirk van Sliedregt (1920–2010). A prolific furniture designer, van Sliedregt was particularly devoted to rattan, pairing curved seat shells that followed the lines of the human body in repose with minimal metal legs and supports. Many of his mid-century modern designs were produced by Dutch manufacturers, including the firms Jonkers Brothers and Rohé.

During the 1950s, design was instrumental in reconstructing the shattered economies of Italy and Germany. In Italy, craft-based industries, such as basket weaving, were well established, which made working with rattan an attractive and affordable prospect at a time of material shortages. In collaboration with Bonacina, the leading Italian rattan workshop, Franco Albini (1905–77), Giovanni Travasa, Gio Ponti (1891–1979), Tito Agnoli (1931–2012), Joe Colombo (1930–71), and Franca Helg (1920–89) all produced outstanding designs in rattan, which showcased the versatility of the material. Bonacina also collaborated with huge success with Renzo Mongiardino (1916–98), the Italian architect and designer of some of the most remarkable interiors of the twentieth century. His timeless designs, such as the Bourlon chair (1940), were treasured by Marella Agnelli, who incorporated many of them into her various houses.

Soane Britain, Mortimer table, UK, 2010.

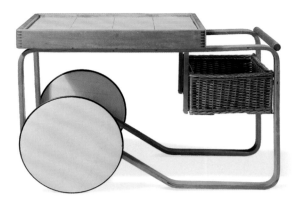

Alvar Aalto, tea trolley, Finland, 1937.

McGuire, coffee-cocktail table, USA, 1980s.

Vittorio Bonacina, Exagonal table, Italy, 1940.

LEFT: Jean Royère, coffee table, France, 1954.

OPPOSITE: The Dryad Leighton table is a scaled-up version of an original design from the Dryad archive and made by Soane Britain. Combined here in my London apartment with Islamic pictures, textiles, and objects, its Eastern form adds to the richness of the room.

PRECEDING PAGES: This atrium, in a nineteenth-century Philadelphia house, was created with blocks of coral stone around 1930, and is now an informal sitting room at the heart of a more formal house decorated by New York–based Thomas Jayne. Inspired by the nineteenth-century practice of wicker furniture being used indoors and out, and using it in many types of rooms, as much for function as for decoration, Jayne's studio has a long tradition of using rattan and wicker in the interiors it creates. This relatively simple set from the 1920s offsets a lunette of frolicking putti and splashing fountain.

OPPOSITE: "What could be more delicious than lots of lovely white rattan by the sea?" enthuses designer Veere Grenney. Renowned for his ability to pair the grandest furniture with humble materials, Grenney incorporates rattan into many of the holiday houses he designs. Here, on Mustique, he combines his own rattan designs, custom-made by Soane Britain, with antique indigo textiles and unbleached linen.

PAGES 122-23: "Wicker is, to me, an essential element in every room. It makes the space feel lived-in, adding that coziness that is so important to me," muses Martina Mondadori Sartogo, whose London sitting room is decorated using warm, earthy colors to evoke memories of Italian frescoes and of her favorite country, Morocco. A mix of inherited and custom-made furniture blends with charming flea-market finds. She decided to include in the mix rattan chairs from her mother's Milanese sitting room (see pages 72–73), designed by Renzo Mongiardino, painting them the identical dark brown and arranging them on either side of the fireplace in homage to the symmetry that the Italian decorator loved so much.

Albini's Margherita chair (1950), Gala chair (1952), and Belladonna sofa (1951) are fluid, sculptural designs—essays in transparency. A play on geometry, Helg's Primavera chair (1967) has a circular seat on top of an hourglass base, a minimal seat cushion serving as a vivid punctuation point. Rattan is integral to the creation of densely woven organic forms of Travasa's designs, such as his nest-like 1966 Palla chair and the expansive 1967 Foglia chair with its sweeping back reminiscent of a traditional hooded chair.

While Charles and Ray Eames, Harry Bertoia, and Eero Saarinen were producing similar organic forms using fiberglass, bent and molded plywood, and metal, rattan was far from overlooked by American designers, particularly in southern California. Often associated with an ethnic or tropical Hawaiian or Polynesian style, rattan emerged as a contemporary material in sleek designs emblematic of a laid-back Californian lifestyle. Tropi-Cal, founded in 1952 as the Los Angeles outlet for furniture produced by the Hong Kong manufacturer Fong Brothers, was foremost in this respect. Danny Ho Fong's Wave collection (1966), a suite of outdoor furniture, used rattan to create folded geometric shapes, wrapped around bent wrought-iron frames. Examples are in MoMA's collection, as is the Lotus chair (1968), designed by Miller Yee Fong (b. 1941), the son of Danny Ho Fong (1915–92). "A seductive well of comfort," as the chair was described in the *Los Angeles Times*, the chair opens out as if to receive its occupant within its embrace.

Although rattan is not indigenous to Japan, there is a long history of rattan weaving in the country. A classic design produced by Yamakawa Rattan is the C-3160 armless lounge chair (1960), which has remained in continuous production since its debut. The first Japanese product to be added to the permanent collection of MoMA, it was created by Isamu Kenmochi (1912–71) for the bar of the New Japan Hotel, Tokyo, and has a cocoon-like shape formed of complex curves. More recently, Yamakawa has produced sculptural rattan creations by Hiroomi Tahara (b. 1977), such as his Fruit Bowl, Relation, and Wrap sofas.

It is too early to judge which of the more recent rattan designs will attain classic or iconic status in the years to come. What is clear, however, is that the material is once again receiving serious design attention. Perhaps a contemporary fascination for mid-century modern may have had something to do with its present revival; equally persuasive must be rattan's unrivaled eco-credentials. Whichever is the case, a new wave of designers and architects, including Marc Newson with his Biomorphic chair, Jaime Hayon, Santiago Calatrava, Alvin Tjitrowirjo, Clémentine Chambon, Piero Lissoni, Tomoko Mizu, and India Mahdavi, to name but a few, are proving to be as beguiled by this wonderful material as their predecessors were.

Style

STYLE

Romantic, and with a certain dreamlike quality, rattan brings understated glamour to both interiors and gardens. Evocative of exotic locations and languid days spent on shady verandas in sunny climates, it invites relaxation. This entrancing informality carries with it a hint of nostalgic charm. It is easy to imagine yourself living in another era, taking tea in a garden room, surrounded by a tangle of palms and ferns, or sipping sundowners on the terrace at Shepheard's Hotel amid the bustle of 1930s Cairo.

Equally, rattan can look entirely modern, stripped of all nostalgia. In pared-down contemporary settings, it can express a more robust modernist aesthetic—clean-lined but with a quieter, more organic presence. Many leading mid-century designers were intrigued by the honesty of the material and its lack of pretension.

Above all, the finest rattan furniture is made completely by hand, bringing the human dimension into play. Unlike mass-produced designs in synthetic materials, rattan is never soullessly uniform, and its woven texture adds a subtle sense of rhythm that animates even the most formal settings. Sculptural and exuberant, or elegant and restrained, rattan's light and airy character makes it exceptionally easy to live with.

Rattan first acquired its cachet as an aspect of chic interiors with the arrival of the interior designer in the early decades of the twentieth century. Arbiters of taste, shaping elegant surroundings for their rich clients, these new professionals—who were often women—set trends that eventually filtered through to the mass market.

A significant forerunner in this field was the American novelist Edith Wharton (1862–1937), whose book *The Decoration of Houses*, cowritten with the architect Ogden Codman Jr., was first published in 1897. In this book, Wharton, an astute chronicler of the Gilded Age in her fiction, was highly critical of the overdecorated houses of the era, filled with overstuffed furniture, layers of light-excluding curtains at the windows, and every table laden with meaningless bric-a-brac. She argued in favor of greater simplicity and authenticity; "willow arm-chairs with denim cushions" for those on a budget, for example, rather than the heavy suites that were mass-produced in dubious styles. The advice Wharton and Codman set out in *The Decoration of Houses* helped pave the way for the emerging new discipline of interior design.

Elsie de Wolfe (1865–1950) was not the very first interior designer, but she was the best known and most influential of her day. Born in New York and a society figure in her own right (she was presented at court to Queen Victoria when she was a debutante), her fascination with interior décor had its beginnings in stage design while she was an actress touring with her own company. The decoration of her residence near New York's Union Square, which she shared with her partner, the theatrical agent Elisabeth Marbury, was revolutionary in its use of restrained color, pretty eighteenth-century French antiques, and the absence of Victorian clutter. Their salon, attended by the cultural elite, led de Wolfe to her first big commission, to create the interior of the Colony Club (1907), in a building designed by the Beaux Arts architect Stanford White (1853–1906). Rather than specify the usual heavy furnishings that dominated public

spaces at that time, she created an airy, gardenlike interior for this groundbreaking women's club, with light drapery, treillage, pale colors, and rattan chairs and sofas. It was an immediate sensation. De Wolfe went on to become hugely successful with a roster of famous clients—from Condé Nast and Cole Porter to the Duchess of Windsor. Arguably her lasting achievement was to breathe a fresh, modern spirit into the home. As she later wrote, "I opened the doors and windows of America and let the air and sunshine in."

By the outbreak of the Second World War, the peripatetic de Wolfe (now Lady Mendl) was dividing her time between a Parisian penthouse and Villa Trianon, her house near Versailles, which she and her husband had filled with superb French antique furniture. Less than a year later, a month before the Nazis entered Paris, the couple fled. After escaping war-torn Europe through Lisbon, and following a stint in New York, they settled in southern California. Now in straitened financial circumstances, de Wolfe, well into her seventies, reinvented herself as a Hollywood hostess, occasional advisor on set decoration, and designer to stars such as Gary Cooper.

The Mendls' house in Benedict Canyon, Beverly Hills, named After All (also the title of de Wolfe's autobiography), was a bravura

OPPOSITE: Manhattan-based designer Tom Scheerer is a devotee of wicker in all forms. He was introduced to the joys of the extra-wide rattan chaise longue ("Perfect for a serious nap without ruffling a bed") by Hubert de Givenchy who incorporated them into his house in the south of France. This house on Harbour Island belongs to Givenchy's nephew, Olivier, for whom Scheerer commissioned this design from Bielecky Brothers in New York. A *morha*, the ubiquitous wicker stool made throughout India, doubles as a side table.

ABOVE: The dining room at Via XXIV Maggio, Marella and Gianni Agnelli's apartment in Rome, for which murals by Mario Schifano (1934–98) were commissioned. Marella employed leading designers, such as Renzo Mongiardino, with whom she closely collaborated, to design her interiors. It was Mongiardino who introduced rattan into many of the Agnelli residences, where its simplicity contrasts with the grandeur of the architectural settings.

PAGE 134: Soane Britain's Venus chair sits in Beata Heuman's book-lined London living room. The Swedish-born interior designer includes rattan, often bespoke, in many interiors because "it's a humble and simple material, and yet requires great skill to manipulate. This combination makes it incredibly chic! Rattan has a certain softness to it which is often lacking in modern furniture. I enjoy using an old-fashioned material like this in a setting that feels current, for contrast and interest."

PAGE 135: Gili Meno, the smallest and most peaceful of the Gili archipelago, Indonesia, is the location of the aptly named Crusoe Beach House. As cars are banned on the islands, guests can enjoy their retreat in perfect tranquility.

ABOVE: Morocco's L'Hôtel Marrakech, in the heart of the red city's medina, was decorated by its owner, Jasper Conran. The marvelous atmosphere is created by Conran's thoughtful combinations of locally made furnishings with antique textiles and furniture such as this vintage rattan seating.

OPPOSITE: African textiles and woven baskets add a relaxed exoticism to Jacques Grange's Portuguese cabana in which rattan tables and chairs abound.

exercise in décor on a budget. The centerpiece of the "party room," with its tented ceiling, was a rattan bar; there was also a large rattan console. Here, in a succession of glittering cocktail parties, lunches, and dinners, guests such as Salvador Dalí, Frank Sinatra, and Hedy Lamarr sat at folding tables in director's chairs to eat, drink, and gossip. Rattan had well and truly arrived in Hollywood.

Whereas the Mendls had fled Paris in advance of its wartime occupation, the French antiques dealer and interior designer Madeleine Castaing (1894–1992) chose the same moment to plunge right into the thick of it, opening a shop on the corner of rue Jacob and rue Bonaparte in 1940. It was Castaing's first commercial venture and one which would eventually bring her eclectic style to the attention of an international audience.

As the beautiful, much younger wife of Marcellin Castaing, an affluent art critic and intellectual, Madeleine Castaing began to develop her idiosyncratic approach to interior design in the 1920s. In 1924, her husband bought Maison de Lèves, a house on the outskirts of Chartres, which she had admired as a child; she proceeded to furnish and decorate it in its entirety. Mixing furniture of various periods and sources, picking out architectural detail in what was soon to be a trademark palette of white, deep red, black,

and greenish blue, she layered pattern on pattern, style upon style. Floors were carpeted in leaf or ocelot prints; white muslin billowed at windows; curious objects and flea-market finds sat happily next to Russian, French, and English antiques. Nothing was pristine and the patina of age (not to mention dust) was positively encouraged. The Castaings moved in a vibrant circle of artists and writers, including Pablo Picasso, André Derain, and Jean Cocteau; they were patrons of Amedeo Modigliani and the expressionist Chaim Soutine.

By 1940, the house had been requisitioned by German invaders, forcing the move to Paris; there was also a new and pressing need to earn money. Castaing's shop, with its striking black-painted frontage, soon filled with pieces from her extensive collection—most of which had formerly languished in storage. She arranged each of the connecting spaces as intriguing room sets, creating the same dreamlike atmosphere that had been so memorable at Lèves. Antique rattan furniture, sourced in Provence and a favorite of Castaing's, added to the beauty of the much-celebrated winter garden. Her interiors, whether at the shop or for her clients, who included

PRECEDING PAGES: In this French Riviera villa, designed by India Mahdavi for a family of art collectors, Mahdavi's Cap Martin rattan armchairs add another textural layer to the sitting room, with its Claude Lalanne bench and Jelly Pea sofas.

ABOVE: The renowned designer and gardener Nancy Lancaster (1897–1994) with friends sitting on rattan chairs in the garden at Ditchley Park, Oxfordshire, Lancaster's home and a favorite retreat of Churchill's during the Second World War. Along with her business partner, John Fowler, Lancaster is credited with creating the English country house look.

OPPOSITE: A hallmark of Jaime Parladé's atmospheric interiors is their unfussy blend of the grand with the humble. This entrance hall in his home in Carmona, southern Spain, combines many of Jaime's most-loved ingredients: colorful ceiling, brick floor, old metalwork, and rattan, to which he was devoted.

Cocteau at his house at Milly-la-Forêt and Francine Weisweiller at Villa Santo Sospir, had a distinct fin-de-siècle atmosphere. It was as if they were re-creations of rooms imagined by Marcel Proust or Honoré de Balzac, two of her favorite authors. As the late interior designer Mark Hampton put it, "She reinvented the nineteenth century." After Castaing's death at the age of ninety-eight, the shop remained open for another twelve years. Her influence on other designers and decorators was immeasurable, with rattan integral to that legacy.

Once a familiar sight in palm courts and on the ocean-facing terraces of grand seaside hotels, where its easygoing comfort was appreciated by generations of vacationers, by the mid-twentieth century rattan furniture's association with the lifestyles of the beau monde was becoming well established. It was no longer simply the marker of a relaxed informality but a seriously chic element of the most elegant interiors.

Rattan played a large part in the interiors of Marella Agnelli (1927–2019) and Gianni Agnelli. She was renowned for her assured taste, seeking out leading architects and designers to create many grand family homes—from the Via XXIV Maggio apartment in

OPPOSITE: The beauty of rattan as a material is that it can be used to express an infinite variety of styles. Soane Britain's rattan Carousel chairs recall a classical eighteenth-century furniture form. The frame is made of steam-bent cane, with a finely woven rattan circular back.

ABOVE: To complement the oversize apple painting in the Palm Beach bedroom of her daughter Eliza, designer Amanda Lindroth chose a vibrant pink for the walls. Rattan, "a must for a Palm Beach abode," fills the room in the form of stools, consoles, and bed trays.

PRECEDING PAGES: Villa Mabrouka in Tangier, known as the "House of Luck," was the home of Yves Saint Laurent and Pierre Bergé from the 1990s onwards. Its interior was designed by Bergé. Elaborate rattan chairs and console table, made in Morocco to a French nineteenth-century design, furnished the dining room. This magical garden pavilion was built by Stewart Church, an American designer who resided in Tangier, and was restored by Jacques Grange. Lawrence Mynott painted the murals.

ABOVE: Strong color emphasizes the graphic quality of rattan, particularly when the framework is open. This suite of antique lacquered furniture adds visual punch to a sheltered, shady porch designed by architect Gil Schafer, while the cheerful color brings unity to the otherwise mismatched pieces that were collected over time.

OPPOSITE: Designer and antiques dealer Richard Shapiro is known for mixing humble, rustic elements with more serious pieces. At his home near Beverly Hills, the poolside portico is a full-scale recreation of the facade of a seventeenth-century Palladian villa. Vintage rattan chairs by Bielecky Brothers are grouped in front of an open fire.

ABOVE: The home at Casa de Campo, Dominican Republic, which fashion designer Oscar de la Renta (1932–2014) shared with his wife Françoise de Langlade, was photographed in 1974 by Horst P. Horst for *Vogue*. The villa, of simple wooden construction, was filled with batik textiles and rattan furniture.

OPPOSITE: A bedroom at Casa de Campo has a rattan canopy bed in a style reminiscent of a Siamese temple.

Rome to Villa Frescot in Turin, along with others in St. Moritz, New York City, and Marrakech. At Villa Frescot, Agnelli enlisted the help of architect and designer Renzo Mongiardino. Here, priceless antiques, objects, and extraordinary art were displayed alongside furnishings chosen for their simplicity and beauty. Mongiardino, who designed atmospheric sets for Franco Zeffirelli's *The Taming of the Shrew* and *Romeo and Juliet*, was a master of illusion and drama. It was he who introduced rattan into the Agnelli interiors. Rattan dining chairs and sofas, designed by Mongiardino and produced by Bonacina, provided a charming, understated contrast to the grandeur of the architecture.

Marella's devotion to wicker was such that she considered it to be a marker of class and refinement. After being shown around the American home of a newcomer to the New York social scene, she said, in an oft-quoted remark: "It will take her another lifetime

ABOVE: The dining room at Valentino's house on Rome's Appian Way. The fashion designer collaborated with Renzo Mongiardino to create the interiors. Oxblood rattan chairs surround the table. Above an oriental chest inlaid with mother-of-pearl is a watercolor by Joan Miró (1893–1983). Mongiardino based the stenciled ceiling and wall patterns on an eighteenth-century Sicilian veranda.

OPPOSITE: This charming bedroom is typical of Tom Scheerer's effortlessly elegant interiors. The white-painted rattan beds came from his client's childhood bedroom and seemed a perfect choice for this Florida guestroom, now often used by her own daughter. The walls are lined in Raoul Textiles Spring Garden print.

All Things Bright and Beautiful

LABRADOR RETRIEVER

THE BEACH

LARE MONEY
Jimmy Breslin

LET'S MAKE MARY

The Last Resorts

The Cousins' Folly

LOVING FRANK

JOAN DIDION

RAGTIME E. L. DOCTOROW

MEG GREENFIELD WASHINGTON

LEFT: Marella Agnelli's bedroom at her villa Aïn Kassimou, in Marrakech, decorated in collaboration with Paris-based designer Alberto Pinto. With walls painted a soft shade of pink, an Italian lace bed canopy, and crisp white linens, the effect is airy and soothing. The rattan chairs are made by Bonacina to designs by Gae Aulenti, the architect in charge of the house's restoration and a close friend of the Agnellis.

FOLLOWING PAGES: A house in Capri, completely rebuilt by Studio Peregalli in the spirit of Caprese architecture of the eighteenth and nineteenth centuries. On the main terrace, a chestnut pergola hosts an *emplacement* of rattan armchairs with a table.

Built in 1959 by renowned modernist architect Richard Neutra, the Ohara house in Los Angeles is now home to designer David Netto. He furnished it eclectically, but with plenty of wicker by European designers such as Franco Albini and Poul Kjaerholm (and out of view, Nanna Ditzel). "I love rattan and wicker because it humanizes modernism," Netto explains. "This architecture is sleek but plays beautifully with things next to it and inside it that are handmade."

to understand wicker." The renowned decorator Sister Parish later adopted the same benchmark of taste, regularly inquiring whether a particular person "understood wicker."

Someone who definitely understood wicker was Rachel Lambert "Bunny" Mellon (1910–2014). Heiress and wife of the financier Paul Mellon, Bunny Mellon created homes in Washington, DC, New York, Paris, Cape Cod, Antigua, and Virginia— all of which became exemplars of effortless style. An art collector, gardener, and self-taught horticulturist, she was a friend and confidante of Jacqueline Kennedy. At President Kennedy's behest, she created the famed White House Rose Garden in the early 1960s. Her decorating motto was "nothing should be noticed." In counterpoint to the highly important art that hung on the walls

ABOVE: *At the End of the Porch* (1918) by John Sharman depicts a young woman seated in an unpainted rattan chair doing needlework, or sewing. This tranquil scene is representative of the early twentieth-century appeal of wicker in America.

OPPOSITE: In this 1948 Horst P. Horst fashion shoot for *Vogue*, the scene is set for elaborate al fresco dining. The rattan sun hat and Swiss organdy dress are from Bergdorf Goodman.

PRECEDING PAGES: Countess Cristiana Brandolini d'Adda, sister of the late Gianni Agnelli, is known for her sense of style. Vistorta, a large estate in the Veneto, was the home chosen by the Countess and her husband, Count Brando Brandolini, to raise their family. The gardens were designed by Russell Page, and the interior designed in collaboration with Renzo Mongiardino, whose first project this was. Photographed by Jonathan Becker, the conservatory is filled with a remarkable collection of rattan furniture with hollow serpentine arms and backs and intricate decorative detail, which are most probably late nineteenth-century American.

OPPOSITE: Mustique, the Caribbean island popularized by Princess Margaret, has long been a hidden playground for the jet set. Obsidian, a villa designed by Oliver Messel (1904–78) for the society photographer Patrick Lichfield and his wife Leonora, was in need of renovation when its new owners acquired it. Designer Veere Grenney respected its airy simplicity, creating beautiful, authentically comfortable rooms. All the white rattan furniture was custom made to Grenney's designs by Soane Britain.

of her houses, she favored gently distressed finishes, unpretentious wicker chairs and tables, and wooden floors painted in checkerboard patterns, with baskets and fresh flowers everywhere. This informal elegance was nowhere more apparent than at Oak Spring Farm, the Mellon estate in Upperville, Virginia, in the heart of hunt country, or at the interlinked pavilions of the Mellon estate in Antigua, designed by the architect H. Page Cross and decorated by Mellon in collaboration with Billy Baldwin.

Billy Baldwin (1903–83), one of the most influential interior decorators of the twentieth century, shared Bunny Mellon's disdain for conspicuous consumption, preferring a classic, yet modern, look that became synonymous with American high style. Comfortable, with an underlying luxury, his interiors were characterized by a distinctive palette of bold color, a layering of pattern, and a well-judged blend of old and new. Wicker was a staple element and one that he handled innovatively: he once claimed to have made "a lady out of wicker." A Parsons table wrapped in rattan was a feature of his

OPPOSITE: The summer drawing room in the Spanish mountain retreat shared by designer Lorenzo Castillo; his siblings, Santiago and Clara; and his partner, Alfonso Fernandez Reyero. Curved rattan benches, bought from an antiques dealer in Seville, sit in all four corners of the room, each arranged around an Italian rattan table.

ABOVE: A bespoke rattan wraparound banquette designed by Amber Lewis for a client's kitchen in Malibu.

PAGES 168-69: The renovation of Villa Saluzzo Bombrini, a Renaissance villa in Liguria attributed to Andrea Vannone, was entrusted to architect Eleonore Peduzzi Riva. She resolved the problem of integrating contemporary design within such a magnificent setting by inserting only a few simple elements. These additions soften the effect of the decorated vaulted ceilings and frescoes without detracting from their classic beauty and importance. The magnificent eastern loggia, Loggia di Levante, approached from the main central staircase, with wonderful views of the countryside and the city, is furnished with simple wicker furniture made in Italy.

OPPOSITE: Designed by Dallas-based Cathy Kincaid, this exotic "shed" was built for her artist client to paint in and dream in. Evoking a cottage in Maine, the floors and walls are painted timber. The rattan furniture by Soane Britain is painted a pale robin's-egg blue.

RIGHT: Detail of a bedroom at Obsidian, the elegant Mustique villa restored by Veere Grenney. Soane Britain made the white rattan bedside lamp with woven shade.

own Manhattan apartment, its walls lacquered deep brown. Among Baldwin's clients were Babe Paley, Cole Porter, Jacqueline Kennedy Onassis, Lee Radziwill, and the legendary *Harper's Bazaar* and *Vogue* editor Diana Vreeland. The living room in Vreeland's 1957 Park Avenue apartment—her brief was that it should resemble "a garden in hell"— had scarlet walls, blood-red floral chintz sourced from the English decorator John Fowler, and red-upholstered rattan-framed chairs.

With many high-profile clients availing themselves of the services of the same select group of decorators, it is hardly surprising that wicker became as fashionable as it did. An insider within the exclusive group, as well as a keen observer of it, was the author Truman Capote (1924–84), at one time a close friend of Marella Agnelli's. Later, they would fall out after the publication of his roman à clef *Answered Prayers*, which fictionalized tales of her social circle told to him in confidence. Like Agnelli, Capote also had an extensive collection of antique wicker, much of it painted, which furnished his retreat in the Hamptons.

Madeleine Castaing was one of France's most brilliant and sought-after decorators, who drew upon an eclectic mix of periods and styles to create her fairytale interiors. She opened her legendary store in Paris in 1940, filling it with pieces from her extraordinary collection. This is a scene from one of her storerooms on Rue Visconti in Saint Germain, arranged as an atmospheric rattan-filled "winter garden."

ABOVE: In this highly colorful and original San Francisco house designed by New York–based decorator Jeffrey Bilhuber, a nineteenth-century Sicilian rattan armchair, one of a set of four, "exemplifies the easiness and uncomplicated sophistication of California living."

OPPOSITE: Tina Livanos Onassis, first wife of Greek shipowner Aristotle Onassis, relaxing by the swimming pool aboard their yacht, *Christina O*, Monte Carlo, 1958.

A designer who had a huge influence on twentieth-century taste, who is somewhat overlooked today, was Van Day Truex (1904–79). Head of Parsons School of Design in the 1940s and later design director of Tiffany & Company, Truex spent his formative years in Paris. His inspirational interiors, most notably those he created in his Provençal houses, were essays in elegant restraint. Natural fibers and materials, including cotton, linen, terracotta, and stone, were combined with simple furniture—much of it locally made in rattan—to create a classic distillation of country style rather than outright rusticity. Rattan also played a prominent role in his New York apartment.

The British society and fashion photographer Cecil Beaton (1904–80) was another devotee of wicker. At Reddish, the sixteenth-century Wiltshire house where he lived from 1947 until his death, the conservatory—or winter garden—was filled with antique wicker.

PAGE 176: The drawing room at Cobblers Cove Hotel in Barbados is furnished with rattan, inspired by the plentiful ferns on Barbados, and custom made by Soane Britain. It is painted Messel green, paying homage to Oliver Messel and the theatrical houses he designed on the island. The glorious soft breezes blowing through the hotel are accentuated by the linen lawn curtains in Soane's Scrolling Fern print.

PAGE 177: Built in 1730, the Hôtel Drujon is situated in Vallabrègues, Provence, and has been the home of Anthony Watson and Benoit Rauzy since 2014. Cofounders of the design studio and workshop Atelier Vime, they sell vintage furniture made of rattan and willow. The design studio also creates its own designs, which include this beautiful Medici vase and pedestal, both made at the wicker-weaving workshop they established at the house.

ABOVE: Fashion designer Diane von Furstenberg having breakfast in bed in her apartment in New York City in 1976.

PAGES 180-81: Cecil Beaton and David Hockney in the winter garden at Reddish, Wiltshire, in 1969. Beaton had worked with decorator Felix Harbord on the conservatory's design to create the heady atmosphere of a Second Empire winter garden with its profusion of rampant scented plants and wicker furniture—the very same atmosphere so loved by Madeleine Castaing.

ABOVE: Mimi Herrera, photographed by Horst P. Horst, sitting on the terrace of her Venezuelan hacienda amid an exuberant collection of rococo rattan.

In one of the bathrooms, there was even reputed to be a wicker commode. Beaton's fondness for a style of furnishing that was prevalent during his Edwardian childhood was not simply a matter of personal taste or nostalgia. He well understood how wicker created an understated yet theatrical backdrop for portraits.

Beaton had brought his passion for wicker to an American audience in 1956 when he designed the sets for the Broadway musical *My Fair Lady*. Subsequently, he would go on to advise on set production for the 1964 movie, as well as to design costumes for both stage and screen versions. Similarly, Beaton's 1912 Room, with its antique wicker furniture, which he designed for the National Home Furnishings Show at the Coliseum, New York City, created a stir among his rich,

ABOVE: *The Convalescent* (1876) by French artist James Tissot (1836–1902), renowned for his atmospheric paintings of fashionable women.

OPPOSITE: The Belgian collector, antiquarian, and designer Axel Vervoordt prizes the innate imperfection of natural materials. The terrace of this Belgian house, where curved tree trunks support a wooden roof, includes a collection of rattan chairs and simple, rough-hewn wooden furniture.

PAGES 184-85: Society photographer Slim Aarons declared his fondness for shooting "attractive people doing attractive things in attractive places." He employed no stylist; instead, his pictures reveal the ease with which his subjects viewed him as he moved about in their glamorous circles. Former actress Princess Patricia Anne zu Hohenlohe-Waldenburg-Schillingsfürst (née Wilder, 1913-95, center), is pictured in 1967 on a shady terrace in Marbella, Spain, with friends including the Marquesa de Villalobar (left).

influential, and artistic friends. During his stay in New York, Beaton furnished his own apartment at the Ambassador Hotel on Park Avenue with pieces from his own wicker collection, including two new acquisitions, chaise longues rescued from the legendary Grand Union Hotel in Saratoga Springs, New York. His famous portraits of Marilyn Monroe were shot in the apartment, with wicker playing a key supporting role, as it did in many of his photographs. Sitters who found themselves framed by wicker over the years also included the British model Jean Shrimpton, David Hockney, and Beaton himself.

The American designer whom Beaton considered most original was Michael Taylor (1927–86), a lifelong devotee of rattan. Influenced

ABOVE: A rattan hammock sways gently in Malapasqua, Philippines.

OPPOSITE: Scalloped rattan designed and made by Soane Britain decorates the Camelot suite at Cobblers Cove, a hotel in Barbados. Rattan lighting is particularly lovely in bedrooms where its mellow diffusion of light creates evocative patterns and pools of shade, which are especially atmospheric at night. Bed hangings in Seaweed Lace printed linen are also made by Soane Britain.

PAGES 188-89: British actor and author David Niven (1910–83) luxuriating in a rattan chair in Saint-Jean-Cap-Ferrat on the Cote d'Azur in 1965.

by Syrie Maugham's famous white decorating schemes of the 1920s and '30s, and by the work of West Coast decorator Frances Elkins, Taylor was instrumental in creating what became known in the 1970s as the California Look. Taylor was especially aware of the changing values of natural light; his interiors, predominantly white, blurred the lines between outside and in, with the inclusion of boulders and luxuriant plants. Furniture was an eclectic fusion of the rustic and the glamorous. Rattan was well suited to his sophisticated yet simple style, and he used it extensively.

When high society morphed into the jet set of the 1960s and '70s, rattan's association with travel and leisure was brought right up to date. Rather than evoke the heyday of ocean liners and steamers or the Riviera at its height, its popularity spread to newly discovered exotic playgrounds for the rich and fashionable, from Marbella to Mykonos. In 1975, Mexican-born socialite and style icon Gloria Guinness (1913–80) and her husband Loel built a spectacular beach

ABOVE: "Add wicker to a room and you add life," advised the influential American interior designer Michael Taylor (1927–86). Inspired by two of the early twentieth-century's greatest women designers, Frances Elkins and Syrie Maugham, Taylor was the originator of a new look in decorating in 1950s California. His all-white interiors were known for their abundant use of overscale wicker, natural wood, and huge plants, as seen here in Taylor's own house in San Francisco, where he has combined a bed made of alder trees with rattan and willow seating and a William and Mary table. In the 1970s, Taylor designed a collection of monumental rattan sofas and chairs in boxy shapes with broad arms for Wicker Wicker Wicker, which were described by the *New York Times* as having a "masculine, even virile, look because they are woven on a large diameter of reed and the frames are so strong and substantial."

OPPOSITE: Vintage linear rattan seats on metal legs surrounding a circular table create an informal eating area in the Santo Domingo apartment of Carlos Mota.

PAGE 92: Soane Britain's upholstered rattan Venus chair adds glamour to a bathroom in an English Georgian rectory.

ABOVE: Belgian decorator Gert Voorjans's interiors are revered for their exuberant mix of texture, color, and period. His own dining room, in an art deco town house in the center of Antwerp, demonstrates the atmosphere with which Voorjans imbues rooms, artfully mixing boldly scaled, antique rattan chairs with a charming and delicate rose-glass hanging light. He loves to use rattan within his interiors because "it brings a very homely feel to the rooms and takes away the seriousness of antiques."

PAGES 194-95: Detail of the entrance hall of a villa in Naples, created by Studio Peregalli. The rattan benches, lined on the wall, are paired with ancient Eastern paintings.

OPPOSITE: This Mill Valley house in northern California was transformed into a family home by architect Gil Schafer and British interior designer Rita Konig, who recalls, "Gil handed me a pretty spectacular canvas with this bathroom. The first thing my client Mark Harris and I worked on was commissioning Hugo Guinness to do that wonderful drawing. It really set the tone for the room. The rattan stool was from a shopping trip we made to Beall & Bell in Greenport on the North Fork of Long Island. Those small pieces are always the things that just finish a room and set them apart."

RIGHT: An antique rattan trolley is filled with bath oils, shells, and a pair of Bidriware rosewater sprinklers in my own bathroom.

FOLLOWING PAGES: The seventeenth-century Château du Champ-de-Bataille in Normandy, owned by Paris-based decorator Jacques Garcia, was the subject of a twenty-year restoration. Inspired by Indian follies and overlooking the water garden, this mogul-inspired pavilion houses a set of rattan seats including a sofa and two elephant-shaped armchairs probably made in India in the 1920s.

house in the hills above Acapulco, designed by the Mexican architect Marco Aldaco. With its curved stucco walls, wicker furniture, open-air living areas, and thatched roof made of palm fronds, reminiscent of a *palapa*, it was the epitome of chic, yet a setting for informal vacation living.

In the immediate postwar years, rattan had been consistently favored by leading designers and decorators, and had played a significant role in forging a distinctly American high style, as practiced by Albert Hadley, Van Day Truex, Sister Parish, and Billy Baldwin, among others. In the relaxed settings of beach houses and

ABOVE: Horst P. Horst's photograph, taken for *House & Garden* in 1970, shows the relaxed covered and curtained patio of his own Long Island house with rattan furniture and a large bouquet of flowers on the round table.

OPPOSITE: Architect Gil Schafer was commissioned to design this charming Southampton house for Lauren and Andrés Santo Domingo. To realize her vision of an old-world sun porch or conservatory, Lauren collaborated with New York–based decorator Virginia Tupker. "Wicker furniture is perfect for lending an air of casual elegance to any room, and it was exactly that easy, relaxed yet refined spirit we wanted to capture here." The rattan designs come from Soane Britain's Lily collection, designed in collaboration with Mark D. Sikes.

country retreats from Nantucket to Malibu, as much as in stylish Manhattan apartments and town houses, rattan was valued for its informality, romance, and relaxed exoticism. McGuire Furniture, a leading American rattan supplier, founded by John and Elinor McGuire in 1948, flourished during that period and numbered among its clients many of the leading design professionals of the day.

By the 1960s and '70s, rattan had reached a new audience. The countercultural movement, absorbed by Eastern mysticism, saw antique wicker furniture, sourced from West Coast outlets and secondhand stores, become a staple of hippie décor, along with Indian print bedspreads and floor-level cushions. It was also resurrected in many of the period-revival interiors where Victorian style, among others, was recreated. At the same time, an increasing appreciation of wicker in academic circles saw antique examples added to the design collections of many museums.

Inevitably, tastes changed. During the latter part of the twentieth century, rattan fell from the cutting edge of fashion once again.

PRECEDING PAGES: Princess Caroline of Monaco, photographed by Slim Aarons, in the winter garden of her house in the palace grounds in Monte Carlo, August 1981.

OPPOSITE: Dating back to the second half of the sixteenth century, the historic Villa Torrigiani in Tuscany has glorious seventeenth-century frescoes by Pietro Scorzini. Mismatched rattan chairs are perfectly at home in the atmosphere of faded grandeur.

Unsurprisingly, there was no place for wicker in the brief interlude of high-tech, or in the minimalist interiors and converted loft spaces of the 1990s. Then, just when its eclipse might have been thought permanent, another shift occurred when mid-century modernism was rediscovered by a new generation. Vintage or retro was the new antique, pattern and color were back, and relaxed informality was the order of the day.

Today, interior designers are increasingly incorporating rattan within their designs to create wildly different atmospheres. From the sleek modern interiors of contemporary yachts to the Japanese aesthetic of *wabi-sabi*, rattan is being combined with soft natural elements as much as with hard-edged metals and glass. Re-creations of the belle époque include antique rattan from the great nineteenth- and twentieth-century manufacturers such as Heywood-Wakefield in the United States, Ellmore in the United Kingdom, and Perret et Vibert in France. For designers who combine the classic with the contemporary, rattan plays yet another role as a humble foil for grander pieces. Natural, white-painted, or vividly colored, traditional in form or boldly asymmetrical, rattan's innate versatility is once again making it a much-favored element in the creation of beautiful interiors.

ABOVE: Marella Agnelli, photographed by Horst P. Horst for *Vogue*, reclines on a rattan chaise longue on the loggia at Villa Agnelli, 1967.

OPPOSITE: Babe Paley, photographed by Slim Aarons in 1959, by the pool at Round Hill, the family holiday home in Jamaica. In the background, her husband Bill can be seen snapping the photographer. The rattan-filled pool house has loungers with segmented mattresses supported by curved rattan frames.

PAGES 208-9: C. Z. Guest (1920–2003) was a socialite, American style icon, and member of a glittering circle that included Babe Paley, the Duke and Duchess of Windsor, and Truman Capote. At her wedding to Winston Guest, a second cousin of Winston Churchill, Ernest Hemingway was best man. Here, photographed by Slim Aarons in 1955, she reclines on a wicker lounger by the side of the pool, with its dazzling white Grecian temple, at the Guests' oceanfront estate, Villa Artemis, in Palm Beach.

Rattan Craftsmanship

RATTAN CRAFTSMANSHIP

PRECEDING PAGES: Soane's Ripple console being woven from the top down.

OPPOSITE (TOP AND BELOW LEFT): Lengths of rattan of varying diameters arrive in the workshops in bales. The canes are steamed in this long boiler to make them malleable.

OPPOSITE (BELOW RIGHT): After steaming, each cane is guided around a machine called a bender and then bent into shape using wooden jigs and another tool, called a commander. These curved pieces are then assembled to make a robust skeleton frame ready to be woven around.

The process of transforming a vine-like jungle palm into sculptural, fluid forms is nothing short of alchemy. The slender-stemmed rattan palm is deceptively strong and extraordinarily flexible, lending itself to the creation of ergonomically pleasing designs—in particular, seating. Rattan chairs are intrinsically comfortable, yielding to the human form and softening with use.

Making rattan furniture in the traditional way, by hand, is extremely labor-intensive. It can take a skilled weaver well over a month to complete a densely woven sofa. Handwoven rattan is markedly superior to machine-made pieces and has the potential, if properly cared for, to last well beyond a lifetime (much of the rattan in my collection is more than a hundred years old and despite signs of continuous use is still in excellent condition). A distinction should be drawn between modes of production and the resulting variations in quality. For machine-made products, the cane is split before machining, which makes it brittle. A good proportion of rattan furniture is made to be transported as inexpensively as possible as flat-pack panels, ready to be assembled and screwed together, further compromising strength and durability. Handmade rattan is infinitely more robust. Difficult to quantify, it has a particular and special quality.

The story of rattan weaving begins in the tropical regions where the palm is grown. The best rattan has no black knots, which would otherwise disfigure the weave, and a uniform density of the inner core. When it is cropped it smells like mown hay. After cutting, it is first sorted and graded by thickness, then it is dried and bundled into bales to be exported around the world.

Knowing how the rattan palm will react when it is worked comes from years of experience; like any skilled craftsperson, rattan-makers will feel in their hands what the material is capable of. The creation of a complex rattan design requires three distinct skills: frame-making, randing (or weaving), and finishing with staining, painting, or sealing. While no two handwoven pieces will ever be precisely the same, which is an integral part of the material's charm, the aim is for each design to be made with as great a uniformity as possible. Particularly when an order of multiples has been commissioned (a set of dining chairs or bar stools, for example) it is essential to strive for a close match of color and weave.

When the bales of rattan arrive at the workshop, they come in a range of diameters: from one-and-a-half inches down to one-tenth

OPPOSITE TOP: Thin strands of rattan, used for weaving, are soaked in small bunches in a tub full of water for up to an hour.

OPPOSITE BOTTOM: Rattan strands are cut to length prior to weaving.

of an inch, and in lengths up to twelve feet. They are graded from A to C, according to knots and roughness. Depending on thickness, the canes, or stands of rattan, will need to be either steamed or soaked in water before they can be expertly manipulated.

The thickest rattan canes—which are used to form robust, sturdy frameworks, the skeletons of the pieces—are steamed for ten to fifteen minutes in a long metal boiler. The thinner canes, intended to be used as connecting stakes within the framework, will take less time. In the hot steam, the cane softens until it is pliable enough to be bent into the required shape. This is done using a traditional wooden forming tool known as a commander, which guides the cane over a bender—a machine with a central steel cylinder operated by a crank. To achieve the correct curvature demands an experienced eye. Bent canes are pinned in position, ensuring they are unable to uncurl, and left for up to a day to dry out so there is no possibility of further movement. The final stage of the frame-making process sees the assembly of all these elements into the required form.

The thinnest strands of rattan, which are used in randing, or weaving, are soaked in small batches for an hour in a tub of water. Randing requires strong fingers; apprentices in the early stages of their training find it hard on their hands. With experience, the weaving becomes almost meditative, akin to knitting, with the fingers acting as the needles. When the rattan dries, each of the strands contracts, giving the weave a strong, taut finish. These thin strands are also used for wrapping, or binding, around the cane frames and joints.

When the weaving is complete, it is time to apply the final finish. First, the hairs on the rattan are singed off, then the piece is either spray-painted or sealed in its natural state. Spraying must be carried out in different directions to ensure an even coating of color. When a rattan design is to be left in a natural state, the canes and strands have to be carefully selected during the making process so there are no tonal discrepancies.

There is an increasingly pressing concern to source materials sustainably and, whenever possible, to avoid all that is synthetic. Rattan grows much faster than timber, can be harvested without deforestation—in fact, it relies on the existence of healthy forests—and is completely biodegradable. Moreover, it supports local communities in the Far East, providing a major source of income and employment. In recent years, the retailer IKEA has joined forces with the World Wildlife Fund (WWF) and other bodies, including the International Network for Bamboo and Rattan (INBAR), to promote sustainable rattan production in the greater Mekong area. This region includes communities in Laos, Cambodia, and Vietnam that are heavily dependent on the rattan trade: in some villages, nearly half the income is generated in this way. Supporting the responsible management of rattan as a commercial crop not only safeguards local enterprise, alleviating poverty, but also reduces the pressure on timber resources.

However, there are plantation challenges for sustainable rattan production, most alarming of which is the competition for land due to the rise in price of palm oil, which has seen the clearing of the standing crop and the plantation areas converted to oil palm. The potential for sustainable cultivation in logged-over forest with the consequent preservation of biodiversity is of real significance and has been the subject of research for decades at Royal Botanical Gardens, Kew.

A growing scrutiny of the origins of everything we buy has highlighted rattan's eco credentials in the last decade, which, combined with an increasing interest in craftsmanship, has created the perfect conditions for rattan's renewed popularity. Fashion, of course, plays a part, but I do not believe that it outweighs the enduring appeal and charm of something that has been made entirely by hand using skills requiring years to perfect and that celebrates the connection between man and nature.

INDEX

Page references for pictures are given in bold

FOLLOWING PAGES: A family transporting rattan chairs and tables along the highway in Sichuan Province, China.

Picture credits

The author has made every effort to trace the copyright holders, photographers, and designers. We apologize in advance for any unintentional omission and would be pleased to insert the appropriate acknowledgment in any subsequent printing.

2 Christie's Images / Bridgeman Images; 4–5 Mondadori Portfolio / Getty Images; 6 © Roberto Peregalli / Studio Peregalli; 8 © Lulu Lytle; 9 James Mortimer / © Soane Britain; 10 Ilbusca / Getty Images; 11 © Wakefield Historical Society; 12 Cristian Barnett / *House & Garden* © The Condé Nast Publications Ltd.; 13 Miguel Flores-Vianna / © Soane Britain; 14 The Montifraulo Collection / Getty Images; 15 Library of Congress / Getty Images; 16–17 Lisa Sheridan Studio / Getty Images; 18–19 Photographed by Joshua Greene © 2020 Joshua Greene / www.archiveimages.com; 20 Bert Morgan / Getty Images; 21 James Mortimer / © Soane Britain; 22 © Christopher Baker; 23 © Roberto Peregalli / Studio Peregalli; 24 © Royal Automobile Club; 25 © Thibault Jeanson; 26 Museum purchase funded by Audrey Jones Beck / Bridgeman Images; 27 Bettmann / Getty Images; 28 (all images) Courtesy of Dryad archives; 29 Alexander James / © Soane Britain; 30–31 Reproduced with permission of Griffith Institute, University of Oxford; 33 © Jaroslav Moravcik; 34 © University of Bristol; 35 Old Paper Studios / Alamy Stock Photo; 36 (above) Gretchen Liu / National Archives of Singapore; 36 (below) © British Library Board. All rights reserved / Bridgeman Images; 37 Courtesy of Dominic Winter; 38–39 Byron Company / Bridgeman Images; 40 © Museum of the City of New York; 41 Heritage Images / Getty Images; 42–43 George Rinhart / Getty Images; 44 TopFoto; 45 Granger Historical Picture Archive / Alamy Stock Photo; 46–47 © Robert Capa / International Center of Photography / Magnum Photos; 48 DEA / G. Dagli Orti / Getty Images; 49 © Historic England; 50 Courtesy of the Richard Marchand Collection; 51 Geoffrey Clements / Corbis Historical / Getty Images; 52 © Beinecke Rare Book and Manuscript Library; 53 Vasili Semenovich Sadovnikov / Alamy Stock Photo; 54 Courtesy of the U.S. National Archives, photo no. NARA_198958; 55 © Alexandre Bailhache; 56 Prismatic Pictures / Bridgeman Images; 57 United Archives / Carl Simon / Bridgeman Images; 58 (above) Sovfoto / UIG / Bridgeman Images; 58 (below left) Camerique / Getty Images; 59 Henry Clarke / Condé Nast Collection / Getty Images; 60–61 © Eric Boman; 62 adoc-photos / Getty Images; 63 © The Cecil Beaton Studio Archive at Sotheby's; 64 Walter Sanders / The LIFE Picture Collection / Getty Images; 65 Image courtesy Titanus / AF Archive / Mary Evans Picture Library; 66 Eric J. Baker / Condé Nast Collection / Getty Images; 67 © Oberto Gili; 68–69 Estate of Evelyn Hofer / Getty Images; 70 Tim Street-Porter; 71 Ernst Beadle / Condé Nast Collection / Getty Images; 72–73 © Massimo Listri; 74 © Christie's Images / Bridgeman Images; 75 Photo © Nicolas Mathéus / ELLE Décoration. Réalisation © Laurence Dougier / ELLE Décoration; 76–77 © Bonacina; 79 Hulton Archive / Getty Images; 80 © Bonacina; 81 Courtesy of Nanna Ditzel Design; 82 (top row, left) De Agostini Picture Library / Getty Images; 82 (top row, center) © 1stdibs; 82 (top row, right) © 1stdibs; 82 (middle row, left) © 1stdibs; 82 (middle row, center) © 1stdibs; 82 (middle row, right) © 1stdibs; 82 (bottom row, left) © Modernity; 82 (bottom row, center), © 1stdibs; 82 (bottom row, right) © 1stdibs; 83 Print Collector / Hulton Archive / Getty Images; 84 © Bonacina; 85 © 2020 Digital Image Museum Associates / LACMA / Art Resource NY / Scala, Florence; 86–87 Sterling and Francine Clark Art Institute, Williamstown, Massachusetts / Bridgeman Images; 88 (top row, left) © 1stdibs; 88 (top row, center) © Galerie Matthieu Richard; 88 (top row, right) © 1stdibs; 88 (middle row, left) © Galerie Matthieu Richard; 88 (middle row, center) © Galerie Matthieu Richard; 88 (middle row, right) © Galerie Matthieu Richard; 88 (bottom row, left) © Demisch Danant; 88 (bottom row, center) © 1stdibs; 88 (bottom row, right) © 1stdibs; 89 © Yamakawa; 90–91 © The Cecil Beaton Studio Archive at Sotheby's; 92 © Modernity; 93 (above) By kind permission of Paulette Frankl; 93 (below, left) © 1stdibs; 93 (below, center) © Modernity; 93 (below, right) © Modernity; 94 (top row, left) © 1stdibs; 94 (top row, center) © Galerie Matthieu Richard; 94 (top row, right) © Modernity; 94 (middle row, left) © Bonacina; 94 (middle row, center) © Tom Dixon; 94 (middle row, right) © 1stdibs; 94 (bottom row, left) © Bonacina; 94 (bottom row, center) © 1stdibs; 94 (bottom row, right) © Soane Britain; 95 © François Halard; 96 © Galerie Chenel; 97 (top) © 1stdibs; 97 (middle) © Bonacina; 97 (bottom) © Galerie Matthieu Richard; 98 Horst P. Horst / Condé Nast Collection / Getty Images; 99 © Anthony Watson / Atelier Vime; 100 © Fondazione Franco Albini; 101 © Tobias Jacobsen; 102 © Guido Taroni; 103 © Ricardo Labougle; 104–105 © Magnus Marding; 106 © Nazuna Kyoto Gosho; 107 © Francesca Ferrari; 108–109 © Trevor Tondro / Elle Décor; 110 (top left) © 1stdibs; 110 (top right) © Modernity; 110 (bottom left) © Galerie Matthieu Richard; 110 (bottom right) © Svenkst Tenn; 111 Slim Aarons / Getty Images; 112 Slim Aarons / Getty Images; 113 François Halard; 115 © Bonacina; 116 (top row, left) © Soane Britain; 116 (top row, right) © Modernity; 116 (middle row, left) © Demisch Danant; 116 (middle row, right) © Galerie Matthieu Richard; 117 © Alexander James / © Soane Britain; 118–119 © Jayne Design Studio; 121 David Oliver; 122–123 Miguel Flores-Vianna / The Interior Archive; 124–125 Horst P. Horst / Condé Nast Collection / Getty Images; 127 © Alexandre Bailhache; 128 Photo © Nicolas Mathéus / ELLE Décoration. Réalisation © Laurence Dougier / ELLE Décoration; 129 © Alex James; 130 © Guido Taroni; 131 © Romain Laprade; 132 Francesco Lagnese / OTTO; 133 © Oberto Gili; 134 Paul Raeside / OTTO; 135 Nikole Ramsay / www.nikoleramsay.com / www.theislandhouses.com; 136 © Jasper Conran; 137 © Ricardo Labougle; 138 Bettmann / Getty Images; 139 Sportsphoto / Alamy Stock Photo; 140–141 © Ambroise Tezenas; 142 Digital Collections and Archives, Tufts University; 143 © Ricardo Labougle; 144 © Miguel Flores-Vianna; 145 © Jonny Valiant; 146–147 © Guido Taroni; 148 Eric Piasecki / OTTO; 149 Lisa Romerein / OTTO; 150 Horst P. Horst / Condé Nast Collection / Getty Images; 151 Horst P. Horst / Condé Nast Collection / Getty Images; 152 Derry Moore; 153 Francesco Lagnese / OTTO; 154–155 © Eric Boman; 156–157 © Roberto Peregalli / Studio Peregalli; 158–159 © François Halard; 160 James E. Roberts Fund / Bridgeman Images; 161 Horst P. Horst / Getty Images; 162–163 © Jonathan Becker; 165 David Oliver; 166 © Manolo Yllera; 167 © Tess Neustadt; 168–169 © Carla De Benedetti; 170 Miguel Flores-Vianna / The Interior Archive; 171 David Oliver; 172–173 Derry Moore; 174 © Trel Brock; 175 Slim Aarons / Getty Images; 176 Miguel Flores-Vianna / © Soane Britain; 177 Joanna Maclennan / The Interior Archive; 178 Horst P. Horst / Condé Nast Collection / Getty Images; 179 Horst P. Horst / Condé Nast Collection / Getty Images ; 180–181 © Peter Schlesinger; 182 Picturenow / Universal Images Group / Getty Images; 183 Simon Upton / The Interior Archive; 184–185 Slim Aarons / Getty Images; 186 John Hale / Getty Images; 187 Miguel Flores-Vianna / © Soane Britain; 188–189 Larry Ellis / Getty Images; 190 Roger Davies / OTTO; 191 Simon Upton / The Interior Archive; 192 James Mortimer / © Soane Britain; 193 Miguel Flores-Vianna / The Interior Archive; 194–195 © Roberto Peregalli / Studio Peregalli; 196 Eric Piasecki / OTTO; 197 © Galerie Saint Jacques; 198–199 © Ricardo Labougle; 200 Horst P. Horst / Condé Nast Collection / Getty Images; 201 Eric Piasecki / OTTO; 202–203 Slim Aarons / Getty Images; 205 © Pieter Estersohn; 206 Horst P. Horst / Condé Nast Collection / Getty Images; 207 Slim Aarons / Getty Images; 208–209 Slim Aarons / Getty Images; 210-211 © Soane Britain; 213 © Soane Britain; 214 © Soane Britain; 216 © Soane Britain; 220–221 The Image Works / TopFoto; 223 © Nilufar; 224 Courtesy of Edwina Hicks Brudenell and Ashley Hicks.

For Charlie, Tom, Bunny, and Xan,
whose tolerance, love, and good humor
have enabled me to research this book.

Acknowledgments

The experience of putting together a book has been more fascinating than I could ever have imagined. I have depended on the kindness of many people, both old and new friends, whom I encountered through my research.

Thank you to Alison Cathie, Elizabeth Wilhide, Lucy Gowans, and Lisa Pendreigh in London and to Charles Miers, Philip Reeser, and Klaus Kirschbaum in New York for their hard work and patience in guiding me through the art of the book. Mitchell Owens has been brilliant throughout, and I am indebted to him for his extremely generous foreword. My heartfelt thanks go to Christy Case and Elisa Shields, whose boundless enthusiasm and tenacity have contributed so much to my research.

I am enormously grateful to the antiques dealers and authors to whom I have spoken, all of whom have so generously shared their knowledge: Suzanne Demisch at Demisch Danant, Sophie Richard at Galerie Matthieu Richard, Eric Marteau at Villa Santo Sospir, Adrien Chenel at Galerie Chenel, Ebbie Koelle at 1stdibs, Modernity Stockholm, Nilufar Gallery, Guy Tobin, and Laurence Vauclair at Galerie Vauclair. On the history of English rattan, I havelearned much from David and Nigel Angrave, Alan Beavon, Tom and Harriet Hardiment, and Dr. Pat Kirkham. For a better understanding of the rattan palm, I am indebted to Alexander Hoyle for introducing me to Dr. William Baker and Dr. John Dransfield of Royal Botanic Gardens, Kew.

Thank you to all of the photographers whose magnificent images are included in the book—with particular thanks to James Mortimer for his unfailing photographic eye, energy, and friendship and to Miguel Flores-Vianna for his generosity of spirit and the extraordinary atmosphere captured in his photographs. Without the kindness of all the people whose homes are shown within these pages, this would be a very different book.

My great thanks also go to Henrietta Courtauld and Bridget Elworthy for their generous encouragement and practical advice at all times and more recently for the introduction to the brilliant Stephen Johnson. Alicia Drake Reece's insightful observations and constant support always spurred me on. Thank you to Maryam Vahidi Kamprad who has kindly introduced me to many rattan specialists in Asia.

Douglas Durkin, without whose fantastic early commissions I suspect our rattan workshop might not have taken off, has my unfailing gratitude. Oliver M. Furth waited patiently for his marvelous commission to be completed as we took over the old workshop, for which I will always be incredibly grateful. I owe great thanks to all the designers, architects, and private clients who place their faith in Soane Britain to make rattan furniture and lighting for their projects.

For their great encouragement, advice, and invaluable introductions, thank you to Chris Albury, Manuel Azpeitia, Katie Aspinall, Adam Bray, Victoria Bridgeman, Emma Buchanan, Rory Buchanan, Caroline Courtauld, Ginevra Elkann, Goya Gallagher, Sam and Hugh Godsal, Ashley Hicks, Katie Hill, Susan Hill, Peter Hinwood, Amin Jaffer, Joanna Ling, Sandra Nunnerley, Rosanna Peel, Dreas Reyneke, Garrison Rousseau, Sarita Posada, Zena Sfeir, Cosima Spender, Guido Taroni, Diego Alejandro Teixeira Seisdedos, Karun Thakar, Chandani Theivendran, Peter Ting, and Peter Twining. My eternal thanks to all my family, especially my parents, Susie and John Kottler, for their confidence and unfailing kindness.

The greatest thanks go to my colleagues at Soane Britain, both past and present, as well as all the brilliant craftsmen with whom we collaborate, who have contributed so much to the establishment and growth of the Soane workshops—with particular thanks to Matt Whittingham for his energy and integrity and to Lucy Whitfield for her vision, tenacity, good humor, and friendship.

Edwina & Ashley

.... go to France and pray

Ashley and Edwina Hicks holidaying in
the South of France, photographed by
their father, renowned interior designer
David Hicks.

First published in the United States
of America in 2020 by
Rizzoli International Publications, Inc.
300 Park Avenue South
New York, New York 10010
www.rizzoliusa.com

Copyright © 2020 by Soane Britain Ltd.

For Rizzoli International Publications, Inc.:

Publisher: Charles Miers
Senior editor: Philip Reeser
Production manager: Barbara Sadick
Design coordinator: Olivia Russin
Copy editor: Victoria Brown
Managing editor: Lynn Scrabis

For Soane Britain Ltd.:

Editor: Lisa Pendreigh
Designer: Lucy Gowans
Picture researchers: Lulu Lytle, Emily
Hedges, Christy Case, Elisa Shields,
Sarah Hopper, and Jackie Swanson
Indexer: Caroline Wilding

ISBN: 978-0-8478-6890-2

Library of Congress Control Number:
2020936617

2021 2022 2023 / 10 9 8 7 6 5 4

Printed in China